A LIFE OF POEMS,
POEMS OF A LIFE

Comtesse Anna de Noailles
(1876-1933)

A LIFE OF POEMS, POEMS OF A LIFE

Comtesse Anna de Noailles
(1876-1933)

Translated by

Norman R. Shapiro

Edited, with an introduction by

Catherine Perry

 Black Widow Press wishes to thank Wesleyan University for its support. Publication of this book has been aided by a grant from the Thomas and Catharine McMahon Fund of Wesleyan University, established through the generosity of the late Joseph McMahon.

Black Widow Press is an imprint of Commonwealth Books, Inc., Boston, MA. Distributed to the trade by NBN (National Book Network) throughout North America, Canada, and the U.K. All Black Widow Press books are printed on acid-free paper, and glued into bindings. Black Widow Press and its logo are registered trademarks of Commonwealth Books, Inc.

Joseph S. Phillips and Susan J. Wood, Ph.D, Publishers
www.blackwidowpress.com

Cover Design: Kerrie Kemperman
Typesetting: Kerrie Kemperman
Cover art: Anna de Noailles, by Henri Manuel, 1928.

ISBN-13: 978-0-9842640-1-8

Printed in the United States

10 9 8 7 6 5 4 3 2 1

To the happy memory of

Caldwell Titcomb,

enlightened and enlightening critic,

constant friend

—NRS

Anna de Noailles ca 1896. Brancovan family archives (with thanks to Eugénie de Brancovan and Claude Mignot-Ogliastri).

ANNA DE NOAILLES (1876-1933)

A poet of undeniable stature, whose reputation has lasted beyond the popularity of her actual works, the comtesse de Noailles was respected, feted, and beloved by *fin-de-siècle* France's literary and lay population alike, counting among her admirers such figures as Proust, Cocteau, Colette, Sarah Bernhardt... even her lifelong friend, writer-statesman Maurice Barrès, whose anti-Dreyfus views in the "Affaire" that divided France ran counter to her own enlightened sentiments. Her official honors included the Grand Prix de Littérature of the Académie Française in 1921, election to the Royal Belgian Academy the following year—the first woman to be so honored—and the most prestigious Légion d'honneur in 1930, of which she was, likewise, the first of her sex to be promoted to the rank of commander.

Seemingly unconcerned with the tenets of this or that poetic school, she tuned the traditional elements of French prosody to her personal lyrical use, refusing however to be straitjacketed by their limitations. Without abandoning its meters and rhymes, she was not against taking liberties with both when the flow of her inspiration demanded; an inspiration often lush and musical, often visual, now synesthetically sensual and even erotic, as much at home in evoking the eternal as in rhapsodizing briefly on the Parnassian plasticity of her cat. Even when, in her later poems, her subjects were the heaviest—preoccupied as she was with thoughts of death and the nothingness that she was convinced must ensue—still, her poetic touch remained light and dextrous. Some saw in this delicacy of style a characteristic trait of the female poet. But Noailles' technique and talent transcended her gender. When Mary Duclaux in the London *Times,* in 1913, called her "the greatest poet that the twentieth century has produced in France—perhaps in Europe,"[1] and when poet Léon-Paul Fargue supposedly referred to her as "our last inspired poet," neither saw fit to modify the word "poet" with the word "woman."

An exotically connected princess by birth, Anna Élisabeth Bassaraba de Brancovan was born in Paris on November 15, 1876, to a Romanian father—the prince Grégoire Bibesco de Brancovan, whose death in 1885 would affect her deeply—and a mother from an old Greek family, daughter of Musurus Pasha, one-time Turkish ambassador to London. Surrounded by artists of every stripe in her mother's salon, she was an avid reader of poetry and writer of her own from early childhood. Her last volume, posthumously published in 1934 as *Derniers vers,* contains nine of her *poèmes d'enfance* [childhood poems], neatly closing the poetic circle of her life, and about which she had herself confided in her memoirs, *Le Livre de ma vie*: "Even then I knew what I was to become..."[2]

In 1897 the princess married comte Mathieu de Noailles, producing, first, a son, three years later, and then her first collection of poetry, *Le Cœur innombrable* (1901). The volume, received with great admiration and recognized by the Académie Française, was followed over the years by over a dozen more, interrupted only by World War I. The success of her poetry, and of three rather racy novels as well, continued despite the dissonant voices of a few dyspeptic critics (Henri Clouard and Charles Maurras especially) as did her active involvement in the salon society of the day. It was only failing health—tangible reason, as it were, for her poetry's increasing preoccupation with suffering and death—that put an end to both. She died on April 30, 1933, and was accorded a state funeral celebrated at the church of La Madeleine, for more than ten thousand devoted mourners.[3]

—Norman R. Shapiro

---

(1) Duclaux, (Agnes) Mary (Frances). "The Countess of Noailles: 'le grand poète'". *The Times Literary Supplement*, 10 July 1913. In *Twentieth Century French Writers (Reviews and Reminiscences)*, p. 178-92 (New York: Charles Scribner's Sons, 1920).

(2) Cited, from her memoirs, in the preface to the 1934 republication of *Derniers vers et poèmes d'enfance*, p. 13. (*Derniers vers* had been published by itself the preceding year, and *Poèmes d'enfance* had originally appeared in 1927.)

(3) As one would expect, there is no lack of factual and critical study of her work. See also the poet's memoirs *Le Livre de ma vie* (1932) for details up to her adolescence. A listing of her principal poetry collections can be found in Jeanine Moulin, *La Poésie féminine*, vol. II, p. 107, and even before her death Jean Larnac had compiled a compendious volume of critical works: *La Comtesse de Noailles, sa vie, son œuvre*. Among later studies one can consult the following: Edmée de La Rochefoucauld, *Anna de Noailles* (a 1976 reprint, honoring the centenary of her birth, of a 1956 publication); Louis Perche, *Anna de Noailles*; the largely archival volume of the same title by Claude Mignot-Ogliastri: *Anna de Noailles: une amie de la princesse Edmond de Polignac* (1986); Elisabeth Higonnet-Dugua's voluminous biography, with correspondence, *Anna de Noailles, cœur innombrable: biographie, correspondance*; and the recent study by Catherine Perry, *Persephone Unbound: Dionysian Aesthetics in the Works of Anna de Noailles* (2003), not to mention a profusion of specialized articles in numerous French and international publications.

TABLE OF CONTENTS

Introduction // 16

POÈMES D'ENFANCE

Mélancolie // Melancholy 29
Le Passé // The Past 31

LE CŒUR INNOMBRABLE

L'Offrande à la Nature // The Offering to Nature 35
Le Verger // The Orchard 37
Exaltation // Exaltation 41
"Il fera longtemps clair ce soir..." // "The days grow long..." 45
L'Image // The Image 47
Les Animaux // The Animals 51
La Mort dit à l'Homme... // Death Said to Man... 53
Chanson du Temps opportun // Song of the Proper Time 55
La Terre // The Earth 57

L'OMBRE DES JOURS

Les Vagues // The Waves 63
Les Ombres // The Shades 67
Attendrissement // Tenderness 69
Émerveillement // Wonder and Awe 73
Le Conseil // Advice 77
La Querelle // The Quarrel 79
La Poursuite // The Chase 81
Les Regrets // Regrets 83
"J'écris pour que le jour..." // "I write so that, when I no more shall be..." 85
"Vous que jamais rien ne délie" // "O melancholic soul of mine..." 87

LES ÉBLOUISSEMENTS

Éblouissement // The Dazzling 91
Soir d'Espagne // Spanish Evening 97
Jour d'été // Summer Day 101
Poème de l'azur // Poem on the Azure 105
La Naissance du printemps // Spring's Beauty 109
Matin lyrique // Lyrical Morning 113
La Nostalgie // Nostalgia 115
Hermione // Hermione 119
La première aubépine // The First Hawthorn 121
Destinée // Destiny 125

LES VIVANTS ET LES MORTS

"Je me défends de toi..." // "Waking, I ban you from my ken..." 129
La Douleur // Pain 131
"O mon ami, souffrez..." // "O my friend, suffer..." 135
"Avoir tout accueilli..." // "To have accepted..." 137
"Tu ressembles à la musique..." // "You are like music..." 139
"Si vous parliez, Seigneur..." // "If you spoke, Lord..." 141
"Mon Dieu, je sais qu'il faut..." // "Dear God, I know..." 145
"J'ai revu la nature..." // "I've seen Nature's beginning..." 149
"Les vivants se sont tus..." // "Mute are the living..." 151
"La nuit rapproche mieux..." // "Night best brings those..." 153
"Je ne veux pas savoir s'il fait clair..." // "I do not care if days..." 157

LES FORCES ÉTERNELLES

Les Bords de la Marne // The Banks of the Marne 161
"Le paysage est calme..." // "Tranquil the landscape..." 163
Matin d'été // Summer Morning 167
"Pour oublier la morne houle..." // "To help forget the dreary tide..." 169
Dans l'adolescence // In Adolescence 171
"Je croyais être..." // "I thought that to be sad..." 175
Consolation // Consolation 177

Méditation // Meditation 179
"Mon esprit anxieux..." // "Anxious, my mind..." 183
Le Plaisir // Pleasure 185
"La douleur est pressée..." // "Suffering cannot wait..." 187
Solitude // Solitude 189
Tranquillité // Tranquility 191
La Nuit // Night 193
"L'être ne recherche..." // "Each being seeks but itself..." 195
"Ni l'éblouissement du regard..." // "Neither the dazzling dawn..." 197

POÈME DE L'AMOUR

I "Ce fut long..." // I "How long it took..." 201
II "Comprends que je déraisonne..." // II "Listen how I rave..." 203
X "Dans les ténèbres de Vérone..." // X "Verona's shades..." 205
XI "Lorsque je souffre trop..." // XI "When your charms shine..." 207
XVIII "Quand la musique en feu..." // XVIII "When music's fires..." 209
XXV "Le silence répand son vide..." // XXV "Silence spreads wide..." 211
XXVIII "On m'a parlé..." // XXVIII "They spoke to me..." 213
XXXV "Es-tu bon..." // XXXV "Are you good..." 215
XL "Aimer, c'est de ne mentir plus..." // XL "To love is to stop lying..." 217
XLV "Ceux qui, hors du rêve..." // XLV "Those who—except in dream..." 219
XLIX "On est bon..." // XLIX "One is good..." 221
LIV "Quand un soudain sommeil..." // LIV "When sudden sleep..." 223
LVII "Enfin la première nuit..." //
LVII "At last, the season's first cold night..." 225
LVIII "J'ai puissamment goûté l'orgueil..." //
XVIII "How staunchly have I taken pride..." 227
LIX "Tu sais, je n'étais pas modeste..." //
LIX "You know, I was not modest..." 229
LXVII "Moi seule je connais..." // LXVII "I alone know..." 231
LXIX "Si vraiment les mots..." // LXIX "If words put you..." 233
LXXI "Il fut un temps..." // LXXI "Time was..." 235
LXXVI "Combien de fois..." // LXXVI "Though many a time..." 237
LXXXIII "Tu vis..." // LXXXIII "You live..." 239
LXXXVI "Aucun jour..." // LXXXVI "Never has it occurred..." 241
XCVIII "En ton absence..." // XCVIII "Without you..." 243

XCIX “Un triste orgue...” // XCIX “A hurdy-gurdy’s plaintive twang...” 245
CV “Sauf toi, tous les humains...” // CV “Save your own...” 247
CX “Sans doute ma vie...” // CX “My life seems duller...” 249
CXIX “Le bonheur ainsi que l’ennui...” //
CXIX “Happiness and chagrin...” 251
CXXVII “Les cœurs purs...” // CXXVII “Hearts pure that ply...” 253
CXXXII “C’est d’une adresse humble...” //
CXXXII “Clever the way I loved you...” 255
CLX “Que puis-je te donner...” // CLX “What might I give you...” 257
CLXIII “J’ai vraiment vécu...” // CLXIII “So long the many days...” 259
CLXIV “Meurt-on d’aimer...” // CLXIV “Does love kill...” 261
CLXXV “Rien; l’univers...” // CLXXV “Nothing, the universe...” 263

L’HONNEUR DE SOUFFRIR

II “Ainsi la vie ample...” // II “Life in its wisdom...” 267
V “Morts qui me fûtes chers...” // V “Dear dead souls...” 269
VI “Ils ont inventé l’âme...” // VI “The soul is an invention...” 271
VII “Ébloui, pur...” // VII “Dazzled, precise...” 273
X “Nul lit, nulle chambre...” // X “No bed, no chamber...” 275
XIV “Vivre, permanente surprise...” // XIV “Life, permanent surprise...” 277
XVII “Chaque être souffrant seul...” // XVII “Each suffering creature...” 279
XVIII “Rien ne me touche plus...” //
XVIII “Nothing can touch me now...” 281
XX “Cela fut, et puis disparaît...” // XX “It was, never to be returning...” 283
XXVII “Des cœurs furent heureux...” //
XXVII “Hearts rejoiced at your birth...” 285
XXXIV “Il convient que l’on appelle âme...” //
XXXIV “We call it ‘soul’...” 287
XXXV “Le jour, hymne silencieux...” // XXXV “Light, day’s hymn...” 289
XXXVIII “Naïvement, innocemment...” //
XXXVIII “Naïve, artlessly innocent...” 291
XLI “J’ai connu la fiévreuse...” // XLI “I knew the feverish...” 293
XLV “J’aurais pu ne jamais...” // XLV “That life must cruelly cease...” 295
LI “Les morts qui m’ont aimée...” // LI “Those dead who loved me...” 297
LII “Le monde épars...” // LII “The world disjointed...” 299
LIV “Silence, mouvement...” // LIV “Silence, movement...” 301

LVI "Je crois voir, entendre..." // LVI "I think I see and hear..." 303
LVII "Dans cette infinité..." // LVII "Limitless flesh..." 305
LXVIII "Univers, je t'ai regardé..." //
LXVIII "O universe, I looked on you..." 307
LXIX "Si ta voix m'avait dit..." // LXIX "Had you but told me..." 309
LXXI "Je suis où tu es..." // LXXI "Nowhere am I..." 311
LXXX "Jadis je m'aimais..." // LXXX "I liked myself back then..." 313
LXXXI "L'homme s'attache..." // LXXXI "To hopefulness mankind..." 315
XC "Je n'avais jamais rien à dire..." // XC "Never had I a thing to say..." 317
CV "J'ai dormi..." // CV "I slept..." 319

DERNIERS VERS

Mission // Mission 323
Reproche // Reproach 325
Obsession // Obsession 327
Résignation // Resignation 329
Contemplation // Contemplation 331
"Le sommeil m'envahit..." // "Sleep rushes over me..." 333
"Les jours ont fui..." // "The days have flown..." 335
Égalité // Equality 337
Chloé // Chloe 339
Chatte persane // Persian Cat 341
Les Îles bienheureuses // The Happy Isles 343
I // I
II // II
III // III
IV // IV
Mirage de Noël // Christmas Vision 351
Sagesse // Wisdom 353
L'Ancêtre // The Ancestor 355
Ténacité // Tenacity 357
Exigence // Demands 359
Conscience // Conscience 361
Conclusion // Conclusion 363
Indigence // Indigence 365
Irruption // Irruption 367

Confrontation // Confrontation 369
Espace // Space 371
Départ // Leaving 373
"Nous ne sommes jamais tout éloignés..." // "Never are we apart..." 375
"Que crains-tu de quitter..." // "Childish and dying..." 377
"Quand j'étais une enfant..." // "When a child..." 379
"Celui qui meurt peut tout..." // "Everything learn the living..." 381

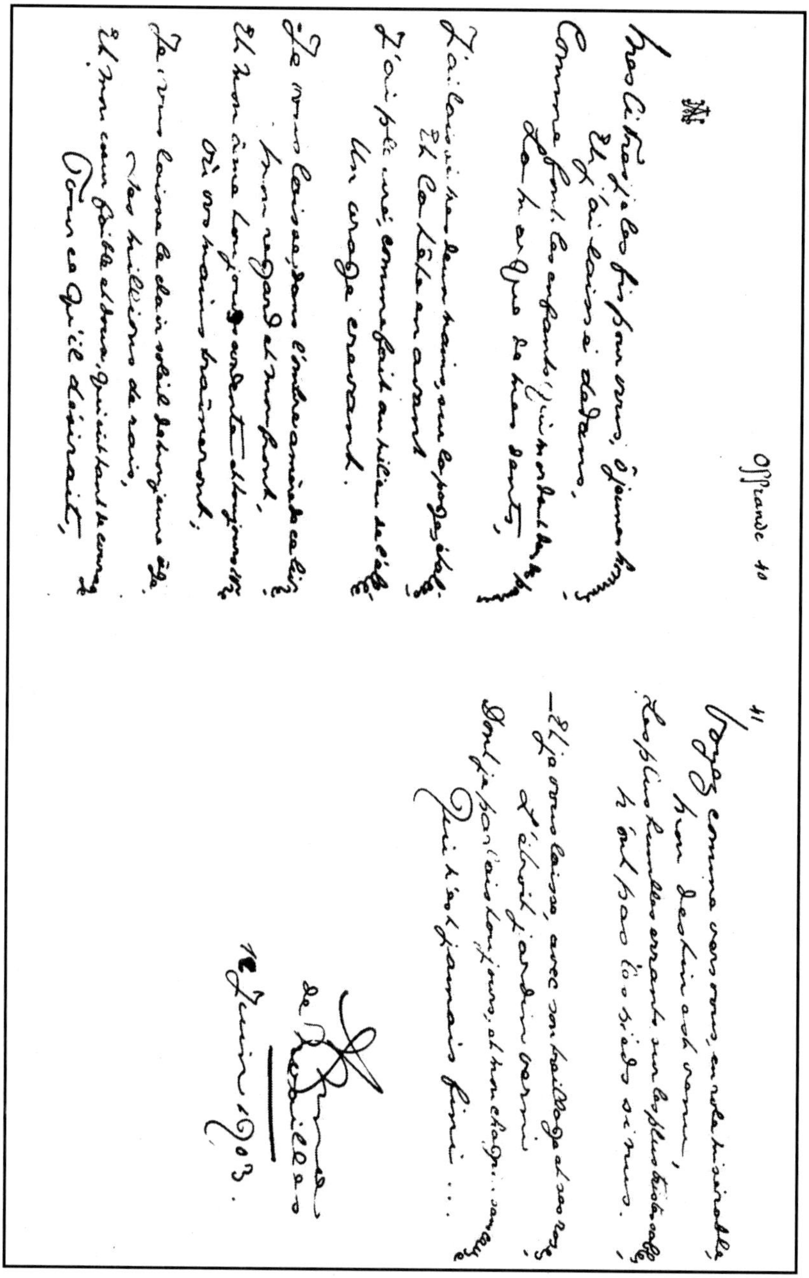

Offrande 40

Mes livres je les fis pour vous, ô jeunes hommes,
Et j'ai laissé dedans,
Comme font les enfants qui mordent dans les pommes,
La marque de mes dents,

J'ai laissé mes deux mains, sur la page, étalées,
Et la tête en avant
J'ai pleuré, comme fait au milieu de l'allée
Un orage crevant.

Je vous laisse, dans l'ombre amère de ce livre,
Mon regard et mon front,
Et mon âme toujours ardente et toujours ivre
Où vos mains traîneront;

Je vous laisse le clair soleil de mon jeune âge,
Ses millions de rais,
Et mon cœur faible et doux, qui eût tant de courage
Pour ce qu'il désirait,

41

Voyez comme vers vous, en robe misérable,
Mon destin est venu,
Les plus humbles errants sur les plus tristes sables
N'ont pas les pieds si nus.

— Et je vous laisse, avec son treillage et ses roses,
L'étroit jardin verni
Dont je parlais toujours, et mon chagrin... sans cause
Qui n'est jamais fini...

Anna de Noailles
12 Juin 1903.

An example of Anna de Noailles' handwriting. Manuscript of the poem "Offrande" (*Les Éblouissements*), dated 12 June 1903 (*Anna de Noailles: Exposition de manuscrits, livres et documents donnés ou prêtés à la Bibliothèque Nationale*, Paris: Bibliothèque Nationale, 1953).

ANNA DE NOAILLES, MUSE AND CREATOR

Among Anna de Noailles' contemporaries, Marcel Proust and Rainer Maria Rilke arguably stand out as the most insightful readers of her poetry. In a long review of her 1907 collection, *Les Éblouissements,* Proust elegantly summarizes the importance of Noailles' work for early twentieth-century literary aesthetics.[1] Looking at the figure of the poet in the paintings of Gustave Moreau, he highlights its androgynous features and remarks that, in the world of his day, this figure is necessarily a woman. Through the androgynous expression "Poète femme" [woman Poet], and referring to the "religious beauty" of Moreau's figure (231), Proust suggests that such a conception of the poet may contribute to a renewal of the genre for modern times, especially in poetry that focuses on the natural world, which for Proust has become the domain par excellence of lyric poetry. In contrast to male poets, who are unable to represent themselves among the natural beauties that they celebrate, a woman poet can legitimately reconnect the body with nature, the lyric subject with its object. In this capacity Anna de Noailles functions not only as feminine character but also as masculine creator. It is through his reading of *Les Éblouissements,* moreover, that Proust introduces the central tenet that will guide the composition of his novel *À la Recherche du temps perdu:* "She knows that a profound idea encompassing time and space is no longer subject to their tyranny and cannot come to an end" (236).[2] This is because the self in Noailles' poetry is not "the social, contingent self" (232) but a self that bears no trace of the social class to which the poet belongs; it is the self that "personalizes works and makes them endure"(233), a self, therefore, that strives to transcend the particular in order to reach the universal. Proust appropriately concludes his review on the poet's aspiration for a territory that would be unlimited. Similarly, Rilke considers that Noailles is able to express a love so vast that it transcends its limited object.[3] As does Proust, he recognizes the dual qualities of receptivity and activity in the female poet, thus her androgynous qualities. He also ponders how Noailles' poetry in *Les Éblouissements* reconciles the self with the external world, most prominently through the body as the subjective seat of nature. In this context, he focuses on the bird as a figure for freedom and the potential for a transfer of consciousness between immaterial space and the sensuous body.

If such interpretations of her poetic work help to place Anna de Noailles back in the context of her literary world, whose aesthetics have become foreign to ours as regards the prominence of set rhythm and rhyme, they also offer us opportunities to recover her poetic expression within the framework of our own preoccupations. On account of her sex, for instance, readers at the time seldom understood Noailles as a genuine artist; instead, they would see her poetry as naively depicting the female self and her body, or as revealing secrets of the "female psyche" for the entertainment, or dismay, of male readers.[4] Because she emphasized the value of the senses, in harmony with an emerging aesthetics inspired by a return to paganism,[5] some critics tended to recognize little more in her work than the received view of woman as representing the instincts and the senses, whereas man represents the intellect. They overlooked revisionary poems such as "Le Vallon de Lamartine" [Lamartine's Vale], in *Les Éblouissements,* and regarded her poetry as a throwback to outdated themes and techniques of French Romanticism. Others saw an expression of confused emotions and unrestrained narcissism cast in unruly language. Perhaps more damaging still, the poet was often perceived only as the "Comtesse de Noailles," a woman of privilege who merely dabbled in poetry and who therefore owed her success to worldly factors.

Though challenged by a number of literary critics, such views have been carried down to our day. This is why Proust's rejection of the writer's "social self," as expressed both in his review of *Les Éblouissements* and in his essay *Contre Sainte-Beuve,*[6] are so crucial for an understanding of Noailles' work. Distinct from the worldly spheres of life, poetry for Noailles participates in a wholly inner and silent world. In 1913, for instance, as though echoing Proust's statement, "books are the work of solitude and the *children* of silence," Noailles describes the conditions in which her writing takes place: "... toujours, je travaille immobile. Je m'offre, de tout mon être, au silence. Il m'apporte mille inspirations, m'ouvre tous les palais, tous les parterres..."[8] [I always work motionless. With my whole being, I offer myself to silence. It brings me a thousand inspirations, opens for me all palaces, all galleries...] In a chapter of her 2011 book on Noailles, Roxana Verona perceptively examines the importance of the cork-lined bedroom where Noailles set down in writing the journeys she took through her imagination, nourished by her experience as well as her extensive readings.[9]

From the time of her earliest publication in *La Revue de Paris* (1 February 1898) Anna de Noailles became the most popular, the most celebrated, and also the most denigrated female poet in early twentieth-century France. Admired by writers, thinkers, and artists throughout Europe, this literary "star" of the Belle Époque was the only woman writer of her times in France to receive the highest public recognition, despite nationalist critics who distrusted her Greco-Romanian origins and could not bring themselves to consider her a legitimate French poet. Noailles' first collection of poems, *Le Cœur innombrable* (1901), was an immediate best seller, appealing to readers not only for the quality of its verse but also for its openness to sensuality from a woman's perspective. Poetry, which had gradually removed itself from the public with the Parnassians' cultivation of art for art's sake and with the linguistic complexities of the Decadents and the Symbolists, became popular again to a large extent through her influence. As Tama Engelking puts it, Noailles "brought pleasure back into reading and writing" (105). Her popularity even surpassed that of Colette for many years.[10]

Starting with *Le Cœur innombrable*, Anna de Noailles published nine volumes of lyric poetry, three novels, a book combining novellas with a series of meditations on gender issues, a collection of prose poems, and, at the end of her life, an unfinished autobiography spanning her childhood and adolescence. She also wrote countless essays, articles, and book prefaces, which demonstrate her lifelong commitment to artistic creation. Recognizing the importance of her work, in 1921 the Académie française bestowed upon her its prestigious "Grand Prix de Littérature." The following year she became the first female member of the newly instituted Belgian Académie royale de langue et de littérature françaises; and in 1931 she was the first woman ever to receive the rank of "Commandeur" in the Légion d'Honneur. Her reputation even extended to the United States where she was nominated, alongside Proust, for *Vanity Fair*'s 1923 "Hall of Fame" (Amory and Bradlee 80).

Although Noailles' popularity decreased after World War I as modernism gained ground with poets such as Guillaume Apollinaire and Paul Valéry, and although her readership declined dramatically after her death in 1933, later critical judgments often confirm that she deserved this recognition. A discrepancy between form and content, reflecting Noailles' position on the cusp of the antithetical worldviews of nineteenth-century Romanticism and twentieth-century modernism, characterizes her poetry, in which dynamic concepts and images strive to dissolve a largely classical structure. By actively engaging with her French literary heritage while also finding inspiration in her Greek heritage and in the thought of Friedrich Nietzsche, Noailles constructed an original poetic world that often emerges as modern in spite of its Romantic trappings and that sets her apart from literary practices of the previous century. The term

"Dionysian" best describes her work: ecstatic, sensual, erotic, playful, sometimes violent, and always marked by a tragic undercurrent that becomes magnified with time.

The present collection of Noailles' poetry in translation accurately represents the variety and breadth of Noailles' work. It begins by showcasing a few early poems, which she composed in part under the influence of Baudelaire and Decadent poets such as Jules Laforgue, Paul Verlaine, and Albert-Victor Samain as well as the philosopher Leopardi (Mignot-Ogliastri 93, 128). Her first collection, *Le Cœur innombrable,* already shows a movement away from *fin-de-siècle* models and constraining forms such as the sonnet. Thenceforth her poetry alternates among a variety of forms, for the most part alexandrine and octosyllabic verse, often set in distichs, tercets, and quatrains, but also in long strophic verse. In contrast to poets who were beginning to experiment with open forms, Noailles consistently upheld traditional patterns of rhythm and rhyme; she did so, she claimed in a 1913 interview, because only such versification could ensure a precise rendition of the poet's perceptions, as well as the reader's participation in her poetic world: "La plupart d'entre ces jeunes poètes négligent la rime, se croient libérés... Mais la rime est la pointe, l'épine, qui accroche, fixe la sensation... La forme traditionnelle et la rime sont comme la palpitation générale où tous les cœurs peuvent s'entendre" [Most of these young poets neglect rhyme, believing that they are liberated... But rhyme is the crest, the thorn, which catches and fixes sensation... Traditional form and rhyme are like the general palpitation where all hearts can understand one another] ("Une heure...," 311).

Apart from a few Hugolian poems on social justice, the main inspirations for *Le Cœur innombrable* were *The Greek Anthology,* Stoic treatises, and works by the philosophers Arthur Schopenhauer and Friedrich Nietzsche, as well as the historian Jules Michelet, along with Noailles' own awareness of suffering and death, based upon early experiences of illness and loss.The conventional theme of the poet's will to overcome individual transience through art is present with a peculiar insistence in her early poetry, which asserts the poet's survival through her verse, often by representing her as nature itself. The opening stanza of the second piece in the volume, "L'Offrande à la Nature," composed in January 1901 (Mignot-Ogliastri 134)[11] and the most applauded poem in the collection at the time of its publication, depicts her as a poet who has loved nature with such passionate devotion that she will remain unequaled. Nature as a divinity grants her the possibility of constructing a poetic identity, an "innumerable heart," unconstrained by conventional notions of gender, nation, ethnicity, or propriety. The speaker renounces reason as the faculty that legislates absolute moral values in favor of an unshackled, animal nature that has become the criterion for her own values. "L'Offrande à la nature" thus embodies several themes that Noailles would continue to modulate in numerous variations over the years. Similarly, the poem "Exaltation" introduces the central value of Dionysian intensity in this collection. Other poems display experimentation with form. In the eighth stanza of "Le Verger," for instance, the near absence of punctuation attempts to replicate the sinuous motion of water drops trickling down a snap-bean leaf. *Le Cœur innombrable* also exemplifies Noailles' originality in granting poetic dignity to mere garden vegetables, a gesture for which she earned the satiric title "la muse potagère" [the garden-patch muse].[12] Not least, the theme of dancing as liberation of the female body begins to appear in this collection, as the playful poem "L'Image" suggests.

Following *L'Ombre des jours* (1902), a relatively somber collection in which nature provides less reassurance and the speaker often appears divided into conflicting selves, Noailles published three novels while continuing to write poetry. *Les Éblouissements* (1907) is the first volume of her mature poetry and the one that had the greatest immediate impact: it went through five reprints in less than two weeks and received more than fifty reviews, most of them laudatory. Among the important themes it explores are reverence for life, energy, heroism (with references to Hugo and Nietzsche), an attempt to recapture the innocence of childhood as the origin of the poetic impulse (which Proust would note), and a predilection for the "Orient" inspired in part by Noailles' background and childhood memories and in part by her friendship since 1903 with the writer and politician Maurice Barrès. Yet the most exalted poems in the collection are directed not to a human lover but to nature, perceived as a constant source of wonder. In her unfinished autobiography Noailles explains her relationship with nature, inaugurated in her childhood, as a mutual one: "je me suis abandonnée à elle et je l'ai attirée sur mon cœur" [I surrendered to her and held her to my heart]; this "passionate union" inspired her to compose a poetry of her own, "une harmonie hardie et neuve, soutenue par la tradition et les réminiscences, mais qui ne recueillait les conseils d'aucune école et ne voulut reproduire que ce qui est vif et frémissant" [a daring new harmony, sustained by tradition and reminiscences, but which took advice from no school and wanted to reproduce only that which is alive and throbbing] (*Le Livre de ma vie* 165).The poet often translates acute perceptions into dynamic and synesthetic images, striving to encounter the natural world through every sense rather than through vision alone, and she gladly yields to an intoxicated loss of control. At the same time, nature emerges as a fearful power demanding the death of individuals for its perpetuation. Adopting the Stoic concept of *amor-fati,* as did Nietzsche, Noailles recovers even the most terrifying aspects of existence through love, which turns what might otherwise be a bitter confrontation with the forces of dissolution into the intense pleasure of an imagined union. Because, in her conception, the spirit is inseparable from the body, several poems illustrate how spirituality is only a sublimation of desire, while others eroticize the sky as though to contest its conventional identification with the spirit. The theme of dance now becomes prominent, as the first poem of the collection exemplifies.

The following collection, *Les Vivants et les morts* (1913), marks a decisive turn from the love of nature toward human love. This volume recapitulates Noailles' tormented friendship with Barrès, who became (temporarily) estranged from her in 1909, while it also celebrates a more harmonious friendship with the poet and philosopher Henri Franck, who died of tuberculosis in 1912 at twenty-three. Both men account for some of Noailles' most poignant verses on separation and loss. New images also appear from a series of travels and prolonged stays in Italy, Sicily, Germany, Switzerland, and the German-occupied French province of Alsace. Noailles' ongoing quarrel with religious dogma culminates in poems grouped under the heading "Les elévations." The Judeo-Christian God often functions as the lyric addressee of these meditative pieces, which led some readers at the time to assume that Noailles had renounced paganism for Christianity. But she had corrected this misinterpretation in an interview with the writer Alain-Fournier in 1911, when the poems had first appeared in periodicals: "je ne suis pas chrétienne. Ou plutôt, je suis désespérée, chrétienne, comme j'étais désespérée, païenne" [I am not Christian. Or rather, I am a despairing Christian just as I was a despairing pagan]. Despite an overabundance of long poems in alexandrine verse, *Les Vivants et les morts* was hailed as a masterpiece.

During World War I Noailles devoted what energy she had to hospital work, while the poems she composed were mostly patriotic and supportive of the troops. But a poet who had so energetically opposed life to death could not fail to be ambivalent about the war, as in the last line of "Verdun," written after a visit in October 1916 to the most destructive battlefields of the war and collected in *Les Forces éternelles* (1920): "Contemple, adore, prie, et tais ce que tu sens" [Contemplate, adore, pray, and silence what you feel]. Likewise, the poem "Les Bords de la Marne" offers a magnificent reflection on death and the perpetuation of life. In her biography, *Anna de Noailles, cœur innombrable: biographie, correspondance,* Elisabeth Higonnet-Dugua reproduces letters from soldiers expressing appreciation for Noailles' poetry, which they read in the trenches and which enabled them to rise, if only for brief moments, above the horrors of the war. Barrès resurfaces as an interlocutor in the final section of *Les Forces éternelles.* Although her love poetry has become more audacious, Noailles' major innovation in this volume consists in titling a section "Poèmes de l'esprit" [Poems of the Spirit], in which she commemorates the origins of her vocation through her matrilineal connection with Greece, as the birthplace of Western thought. Other poems, such as "Dans l'adolescence," endeavor to provide formerly silent feminine figures with voice and presence, while yet others claim to speak on behalf of women.

A sequence of short, untitled poems published as *Poème de l'amour* in 1924 reveal an evolution both in Noailles' inspiration and in her poetic practice: breaking away from the cult of nature and its accompanying Dionysian frenzy, the poems have become laconic and often end with epigrammatic twists that exemplify a new, demystified self. Poem CX is representative of this shift, as the poet stops her course to focus on the beloved, even while regretting the gods and the "azure" that she has left behind. Other poems depict in strong terms the cruelty of love. Apart from readers such as the writer François Mauriac, who declared that the "incomparable dimension in this poet is not her sensibility... but her intelligence,"[13] this shift bewildered Noailles' public. Yet it signaled a decisive turn: in the last months of 1923 her mother and two of her most intimate friends, including Barrès, had died. From then on she composed more than a hundred poems concentrating almost exclusively on death, most of which were collected in *L'Honneur de souffrir* (1927), the remainder appearing posthumously in *Derniers vers* (1933), along with a few earlier poems, such as "Les Îles bienheureuses." Adopting Antigone as her model in *L'Honneur de souffrir* and gazing on the graves of those who have preceded her, the poet strives to identify with the dead and rejects her own life, as poem VI illustrates so well. Some of these later poems present variations on the theme of the beloved's faithlessness, this time lost to death. Others, such as poem XXXIV, shed new light on the notion that the body and the spirit are one. Throughout, the poet remains a witness, as in poem LXVIII, where the translation of the final line, "And I prevail!," perfectly captures her defiant mood and the extraordinary energy that continues to permeate Noailles' poetry to this day. As this final example shows, Norman Shapiro's translations fully respect the spirit of Noailles' original verse throughout this anthology, even as they become new poetic creations.

–Catherine Perry

I gratefully acknowledge Bucknell University Press and the Associated University Presses for permission to use excerpts from my book *Persephone Unbound: Dionysian Aesthetics in the Works of Anna de Noailles* (2003), the Gale Group for permission to use excerpts from my essay "Anna de Noailles" (2002), and Berghahn Books for permission to use excerpts from my essay "Sensual Deviations and Verbal Abuse: Anna de Noailles in the Critic's Eye" (2006).

(1) Entitled "Les Éblouissements," this article appeared in *Le Figaro*'s *Supplément littéraire* (15 June 1907). Unless otherwise noted, all translations in this introduction are mine.

(2) According to Luc Fraisse, Noailles played the role of "midwife" for Proust's work (*Proust au miroir de sa correspondance* 207; see also his more recent articles on Proust and Noailles, listed in the bibliography). Jean-Yves Tadié observes that Noailles was at the origin of Proust's fundamental aesthetic insights: "It has not been sufficiently noticed: Proust sketched the aesthetics of *Le Temps retrouvé* (Time regained) with Anna de Noailles in mind" (403). On Proust and Noailles, see also William Carter's biography, *Marcel Proust: A Life,* and my article "Flagorneur ou ébloui? Proust lecteur d' Anna de Noailles."

(3) See *Die Bücher einer Liebenden* (1907) (The books of a female lover), translated into French as *Les Livres d'une amoureuse,* and the annotations in Rilke's personal copy of *Les Éblouissements,* kept at Harvard University's Houghton Library. Further information on the literary relationship between Anna de Noailles and Rilke may be found in my forthcoming article, "Anna de Noailles et Rilke: des affinités électives?"

(4) See, for instance, Charles Maurras's 1903 study of female poets, "Le Romantisme féminin: allégorie du sentiment désordonné," 225; Jules Bertaut's 1909 book, *La Littérature féminine d'aujourd'hui,* 16-17; or José Ortega y Gasset's 1923 essay, "La Poesía de Ana de Noailles," 429-35.

(5) As Roger Charbonnel explained in his 1909 article entitled "La Renaissance du Paganisme" [The Rebirth of Paganism], "the body no longer appears as the contemptible instrument of sin but as the primary source of all our joys and even as the necessary condition for all aesthetics, combining harmoniously experienced sensations rather than lifeless ideas" (32).

(6) "[A] book is a product of a different *self* from the self we manifest in our habits, in our social life, in our vices" (*By Way of Sainte-Beuve,* 76; see *Contre Sainte-Beuve,* 127.) This essay was published for the first time in 1954.

(7) *By Way of Sainte-Beuve,* 198; see *Contre Sainte-Beuve,* 309.

(8) Noailles, "Une heure chez Mme de Noailles," 310. In her biography, Claude Mignot-Ogliastri underscores Noailles' "extraordinary power of *solitude,* of doubt, of reverie, of imagination" (100), whose origin she traces to experiences of physical suffering and psychological distress during the poet's childhood and adolescence.

(9) Roxana Verona, *Parcours francophones: Anna de Noailles et sa famille culturelle,* 203-38. It was Noailles who suggested to Proust that he line the walls of his bedroom with cork in order to find the silence he needed for literary creation.

(10) Following a referendum in 1924, the journal *Ève* proclaimed Noailles "Princess of Letters," for instance.

(11) In January 1901 Noailles was undergoing forced psychiatric care for "hysteria" at the clinic of the neurologist Paul Sollier in Paris (Perry, *Persephone Unbound,* 233-37).

(12) See, for instance, Jean-Jacques Lévêque, *Les Années de la Belle Époque, 1890-1914,* 87.

(13) François Mauriac, "*Poème de l'amour,* par la comtesse de Noailles," *Nouvelle Revue Française* 133 (1 Oct. 1924): 486.

Works Cited

Amory, Cleveland, and Frederic Bradlee, eds. "Nominated for the Hall of Fame: 1923, the Comtesse de Noailles... Marcel Proust." *Vanity Fair: Selections from America's Most Memorable Magazine. A Cavalcade of the 1920s and 1930s.* New York: Viking Press, 1960, 80.

Bertaut, Jules. *La Littérature féminine d'aujourd'hui.* Paris: Librairie des Annales Politiques et Littéraires, 1909.

Carter, William C. *Marcel Proust: A Life.* New Haven: Yale University Press, 2000.

Charbonnel, Roger [Jean Ferval]. "La Renaissance du paganisme." *Akademos: Revue mensuelle d'art libre et de critique* 1 (15 Jan. 1909): 26-33.

Engelking, Tama Lea. "Anna de Noailles." *French Women Writers: A Bio-Bibliographical Source Book,* ed. Eva Martin Sartori and Dorothy Wynne Zimmerman. New York: Greenwood Press, 1991. 335-45.

Fraisse, Luc. "L'Amitié épistolaire de Proust et d'Anna de Noailles ou la *Recherche* avant la *Recherche.*" lère partie, *Revue de l'Aire* 32 (2006): 157-80. 2e partie, *Revue de l'Aire* 33 (2007): 129-48.

——. *Proust au miroir de sa correspondance.* Paris: SEDES, 1996.

Higonnet-Dugua, Élisabeth. *Anna de Noailles, cœur innombrable: biographie, correspondance.* Paris: Michel de Maule, 1989.

Lévêque, Jean-Jacques. *Les Années de la Belle Époque,* 1890-1914. Paris: ACR Édition Internationale, 1991.

Mauriac, François. "Poème de l'amour, par la comtesse de Noailles." *Nouvelle Revue Française* 133 (1 Oct. 1924): 486-89.

Maurras, Charles. "Le Romantisme féminin: allégorie du sentiment désordonné." (Minerva, 1 May 1903.) *L'Avenir de l'intelligence.* Paris: Flammarion, 1927. 145-234.

Mignot-Ogliastri, Claude. *Anna de Noailles: une amie de la Princesse Edmond de Polignac*. Paris: Méridiens-Klincksieck, 1986.

Noailles, Anna Élisabeth de. *Le Livre de ma vie*. 1932. Ed. François Broche. Paris: Éditions Bartillat, 2008.

——. "Une heure chez Mme de Noailles." Interview by André Arnyvelde. *Annales Politiques et Littéraires* 1555 (13 Apr. 1913): 310-11.

Ortega y Gasset, José. "La Poesía de Ana de Noailles." (*Revista de Occidente* 1, July 1923.) *Obras completas*, vol. 3. Madrid: *Revista de Occidente*, 1963. 429-35.

Perry, Catherine. "Anna de Noailles." *Modern French Poets*. Ed. Jean-François Leroux. Detroit: Gale Group, 2002. *Dictionary of Literary Biography*, vol. 258. 297-310.

——. "Flagorneur ou ébloui? Proust lecteur d'Anna de Noailles." *Bulletin Marcel Proust* 49 (1999): 37-53.

——. *Persephone Unbound: Dionysian Aesthetics in the Works of Anna de Noailles*. Lewisburg: Bucknell University Press; London: Associated University Presses, 2003.

——. "Sensual Deviations and Verbal Abuse: Anna de Noailles in the Critic's Eye." *A Belle Époque? Women and Feminism in French Society and Culture 1890-1910*. Ed. Diana Holmes and Carrie Tarr. Polygons: Cultural Diversities and Intersections. Oxford: Berghahn Books, 2006. 239-51.

Proust, Marcel. *By Way of Sainte-Beuve*. Trans. Sylvia Townsend Warner. London: Chatto & Windus, 1958. Originally published as *Contre Sainte-Beuve* (1954; Reprint, Folio, Paris: Gallimard, 1997).

——. "Les Éblouissements." *Essais et articles*. Folio Essais. Paris: Gallimard, 1994. 229-41.

Rilke, Rainer Maria. *Les Livres d'une amoureuse*. 1907. Trans. Rémy Colombat. *Œuvres en prose: Récits et essais*. Ed. Claude David. La Pléiade. Paris: Gallimard, 1993. 977-80.

Verona, Roxana. *Parcours francophones: Anna de Noailles et sa famille culturelle*. Paris: Honoré Champion, 2011.

POÈMES D'ENFANCE

(1927)

MÉLANCOLIE

C'est l'heure bienveillante et discrète du soir,
Le vieux sonneur monté dans l'antique tourelle
Berce pieusement le vibrant encensoir;
Sur le ciel clair l'église étend son ombre frêle,

Les oiseaux sous son toit ont bâti leur manoir.
Mais voici qu'au travers de la rude dentelle
Ils fuient craintifs, au son que l'airain fait pleuvoir,
Le pignon vermoulu que l'âge démantèle.

Éparpillant dans l'air ses battements dolents,
La cloche éveille en moi des souvenirs troublants,
Sa houle pesamment me frôle et me transperce.

Et dans mon cœur profond, où son écho frémit,
Chaque vibration effarouche et disperse
Un tourbillon d'oiseaux qui s'étaient endormis!

MELANCHOLY

It's evening's gentle hour, discrete, and he–
Old ringer–climbs the ancient tower, high,
Cradles the trembling censer piously;
Church-shadows, frail, profile the bright-lit sky.

The birds have taken up their tenancy
Under the eaves, in twig-laced nest, but fly,
Fearful, when rains the brass sound-shower, and flee
The worm-worn cornice that age rips awry.

Strewing its beats about, the tolling bell
Wakes in me doleful memories with each knell;
The waves roll, heavy, over me and through.

And, in my soul, where quake the echoes deep
Within me, every peel frightens anew
A flock of birds blown fluttering from their sleep.

LE PASSÉ

J'ai peur des lendemains de fête et de plaisir,
Je ne suis pas de ceux qu'un souvenir enchante,
Et le bien dont mon cœur a dû se dessaisir
Est un mort sans linceul dont le regard me hante.

Celui qui goûtera le fruit qu'il put choisir
Ne saura plus l'émoi dont s'enivrait l'attente,
Et mieux que les refus vous blessez le désir,
Baisers, haltes d'amour sur la rapide pente!

L'été vert, enfoui sous les effeuillaisons,
Attriste, d'un rappel, nos sombres horizons,
Nappes de sable morne épandu sans clémence;

Et j'ai l'abattement, moi qui rêve à jadis,
Du voyageur entrant dans le désert immense,
Après avoir quitté la dernière oasis...

THE PAST

I fear days after feast and fête. Not one
Am I whom gay rememberings entrance;
And pleasure I must lose, once it is done,
Is like a shroudless corpse that haunts my glance.

He who will taste his chosen fruit knows none
Of waiting's lust... O kisses that love grants–
Brief halts along the downward slope outspun–
You wound more than refusals' petulance.

Leaf-buried summer, green beneath the trees,
Saddens, with dark-horizoned memories,
Great somber sheets of sand... And I, downcast,

Stand musing, dreaming of life past-bereft,
Sad traveler entering the desert vast,
After the last oasis has been left...

LE CŒUR INNOMBRABLE

(1901)

L'OFFRANDE À LA NATURE

Nature au cœur profond sur qui les cieux reposent,
Nul n'aura comme moi si chaudement aimé
La lumière des jours et la douceur des choses,
L'eau luisante et la terre où la vie a germé.

La forêt, les étangs et les plaines fécondes
Ont plus touché mes yeux que les regards humains,
Je me suis appuyée à la beauté du monde
Et j'ai tenu l'odeur des saisons dans mes mains.

J'ai porté vos soleils ainsi qu'une couronne
Sur mon front plein d'orgueil et de simplicité.
Mes jeux ont égalé les travaux de l'automne
Et j'ai pleuré d'amour aux bras de vos étés.

Je suis venue à vous sans peur et sans prudence
Vous donnant ma raison pour le bien et le mal,
Ayant pour toute joie et toute connaissance
Votre âme impétueuse aux ruses d'animal.

Comme une fleur ouverte où logent des abeilles
Ma vie a répandu des parfums et des chants,
Et mon cœur matineux est comme une corbeille
Qui vous offre du lierre et des rameaux penchants.

Soumise ainsi que l'onde où l'arbre se reflète,
J'ai connu les désirs qui brûlent dans vos soirs
Et qui font naître au cœur des hommes et des bêtes
La belle impatience et le divin vouloir.

Je vous tiens toute vive entre mes bras, Nature!
Ah! faut-il que mes yeux s'emplissent d'ombre un jour,
Et que j'aille au pays sans vent et sans verdure
Que ne visitent pas la lumière et l'amour...

THE OFFERING TO NATURE

Deep-hearted Nature, heaven-mantled, none
Can have loved more than I, passionately,
The light of day, the objects—every one—
Life-sprouting soil, the glistening of the sea.

My eyes dwelt on the woods, the ponds; and worth
More than the gaze of man, the fertile lands;
Leaning upon the beauties of the earth,
I held the seasons' odors in my hands.

I wore your suns, crown-like, on brow held high
In stance simple but no less proud thereof.
My pastimes were your autumns' chores, and I,
Arm in arm with your summers, wept for love.

I came to you, rash, reckless, trusting you
For all my good or ill, finding in them
My conscious joy at what your soul might do,
Brash, with many a beast-like stratagem.

Like flower unfurled, whither the bees fly, drawn,
My life has spread its songs, its scents arraying;
And, nosegay-like, my heart, before the dawn,
Offers you ivy-gifts and palm fronds swaying.

Like stream by trees' reflection hemmed, I know
The lusts that flame your evenings with their burning,
And spawn in men's and beasts' hearts here below
A lovely longing and a heavenly yearning.

Nature, I hold you, living, tight-caressed!
Ah! Must my eyes, one day, be filled with night,
In land of wind and verdure dispossessed,
Ever unvisited by love and light...

LE VERGER

Dans le jardin, sucré d'œillets et d'aromates,
Lorsque l'aube a mouillé le serpolet touffu,
Et que les lourds frelons, suspendus aux tomates,
Chancellent, de rosée et de sève pourvus,

Je viendrai, sous l'azur et la brume flottante,
Ivre du temps vivace et du jour retrouvé;
Mon cœur se dressera comme le coq qui chante
Insatiablement vers le soleil levé.

L'air chaud sera laiteux sur toute la verdure,
Sur l'effort généreux et prudent des semis;
Sur la salade vive et le buis des bordures,
Sur la cosse qui gonfle et qui s'ouvre à demi;

La terre labourée où mûrissent les graines
Ondulera, joyeuse et douce, à petits flots,
Heureuse de sentir dans sa chair souterraine
Le destin de la vigne et du froment enclos.

Des brugnons roussiront sur leurs feuilles, collées
Au mur où le soleil s'écrase chaudement;
La lumière emplira les étroites allées
Sur qui l'ombre des fleurs est comme un vêtement.

Un goût d'éclosion et de choses juteuses
Montera de la courge humide et du melon,
Midi fera flamber l'herbe silencieuse,
Le jour sera tranquille, inépuisable et long.

Et la maison, avec sa toiture d'ardoises,
Laissant sa porte sombre et ses volets ouverts,
Respirera l'odeur des coings et des framboises
Éparse lourdement autour des buissons verts.

THE ORCHARD

When, in the orchard lush and savory,
Dawn moistens tufts of thyme with sap and dew;
When pinks waft sweet; when wasps hang heavily,
Quivering on tomato vines, I too,

Amid shroud-mists, beneath the azure skies,
Shall stand, drunk with the season, with the day's
Fresh light; my heart, sun-thirsting cock, will rise
Insatiable, to sing day's newborn rays,

The warm, milky pale air will overspread
Green seedlings in their vast endeavoring,
Green salad-leaves, paths boxwood-garlanded,
Green pods swelling with life, half-opening;

The furrowed earth—where planted seeds grow, thrive—
In happy, gentle billows will begin
To sense the joy of feeling sprout, alive,
The future vine and grain, sown deep within.

Leaves pressed against the wall, ripe nectarines
Will ruddy glow when bursting sun will strike;
Light will bathe full the narrow in-betweens,
Covered by blossom-shadows, garment-like.

A taste of budding life, of juice-rich fruit,
Will rise from squash and melon, fresh bedewed;
Noon will ignite to flame the grasses mute;
Day will last, endless, in poised attitude.

And the house, with its slate roof, stands serene:
Open, its doorway dark, its shutters, whence,
Scattered heavy about the bushes green,
It breathes the raspberrys' and the quinces' scents.

Mon cœur, indifférent et doux, aura la pente
Du feuillage flexible et plat des haricots
Sur qui l'eau de la nuit se dépose et serpente
Et coule sans troubler son rêve et son repos.

Je serai libre enfin de crainte et d'amertume,
Lasse comme un jardin sur lequel il a plu,
Calme comme l'étang qui luit dans l'aube et fume,
Je ne souffrirai plus, je ne penserai plus,

Je ne saurai plus rien des choses de ce monde,
Des peines de ma vie et de ma nation,
J'écouterai chanter dans mon âme profonde
L'harmonieuse paix des germinations.

Je n'aurai pas d'orgueil, et je serai pareille,
Dans ma candeur nouvelle et ma simplicité,
À mon frère le pampre et ma sœur la groseille
Qui sont la jouissance aimable de l'été;

Je serai si sensible et si jointe à la terre
Que je pourrai penser avoir connu la mort,
Et me mêler, vivante, au reposant mystère
Qui nourrit et fleurit les plantes par les corps.

Et ce sera très bon et très juste de croire
Que mes yeux ondoyants sont à ce lin pareils,
Et que mon cœur, ardent et lourd, est cette poire
Qui mûrit doucement sa pelure au soleil...

My heart, in its insouciance mild, will bend,
Flat as a snap-bean leaf, and nod until
Night's droplets snake a trickle, end to end,
Gently, letting it sleep and dream its fill.

Bitter no more, free at last of my fears;
Weary, staid as a garden wet with rain,
Or mist-smoked pond as dawn's first glow appears;
No more to think, no more to know the pain,

The suffering of the world's travails—the earth's,
My country's, or my own... Only to know
The peaceful harmony of life's rebirths
Sung deep in my soul's calm pianissimo.

All false pride gone, I shall be like the vine,
The currant, artless and ingenuous
Creatures unspoiled, brother and sister mine,
Who work their passion's summer-love on us.

Then I, so touched, so much of earth shall be,
That I shall even think to have seen death,
And, living, join the quiet mystery
That blooms the plants with flesh's dying breath.

And right and good will it be to compare
My eyes to that flax-flower shimmering,
And my heart—heavy, burning—to that pear
In its sun-ripened skin, soft, glimmering...

EXALTATION

Le goût de l'héroïque et du passionnel
Qui flotte autour des corps, des sons, des foules vives,
Touche avec la brûlure et la saveur du sel
Mon cœur tumultueux et mon âme excessive...

Loin des simples travaux et des soucis amers,
J'aspire hardiment la chaude violence
Qui souffle avec le bruit et l'odeur de la mer;
Je suis l'air matinal d'où s'enfuit le silence;

L'aurore qui renaît dans l'éblouissement,
La nature, le bois, les houles de la rue
M'emplissent de leurs cris et de leurs mouvements;
Je suis comme une voile où la brise se rue.

Ah! vivre ainsi les jours qui mènent au tombeau;
Avoir le cœur gonflé comme le fruit qu'on presse
Et qui laisse couler son arome et son eau;
Loger l'espoir fécond et la claire allégresse!

Serrer entre ses bras le monde et ses désirs,
Comme un enfant qui tient une bête retorse,
Et qui, mordu, saignant, est ivre du plaisir
De sentir contre soi sa chaleur et sa force!

Accoutumer ses yeux, son vouloir et ses mains
À tenter le bonheur que le risque accompagne;
Habiter le sommet des sentiments humains
Où l'air est âpre et vif comme sur la montagne!

Être ainsi que la lune et le soleil levant
Les hôtes du jour d'or et de la nuit limpide;
Être le bois touffu qui lutte dans le vent
Et les flots écumeux que l'ouragan dévide!

EXALTATION

The taste—heroic, passionate—that hangs
About sounds, bodies, thronging masses, presses
Its burning touch and its salt-biting pangs
On my heart's chaos and my soul's excesses...

Far from life's simple chores and bitter woes,
Bold, I inhale the odor of the sea's
Warm breath, brash in its violent, noisy throes;
I am the morning air whence silence flees;

Day, dazzling in the dawn's rebirth, the wood,
Nature, the street-tide rushing, bustle-dinned,
All fill me with their turbulence; I could
Be a ship's sail, swelled by the gushing wind,

Ah! To live thus the days that graveward go;
With swollen heart, like a fruit ripe to press
And that will let its juice and fragrance flow;
To harbor fecund hope, bright happiness!

To seize the world and one's desires, caressed
Like a child with a restive beast, and who,
Bitten and bloody, clasps it to his breast,
Drunk on the heat and strength that thrill him through!

To teach one's eyes, hands, will to chance the risk
Joy brings; to haunt life's passion-crest, and try
To breathe the sting of air, heady and brisk,
Atop the mountain summit reaching high.

To be like rising sun and moon, the hosts
Of gilded day and crystal night; to be
The wind-spanned tanglewood; and on the coast's
Broad strand, spun foam, hurricane's panoply!

La joie et la douleur sont de grands compagnons,
Mon âme qui contient leurs battements farouches
Est comme une pelouse où marchent des lions...
J'ai le goût de l'azur et du vent dans la bouche.

Et c'est aussi l'extase et la pleine vigueur
Que de mourir un soir, vivace, inassouvie,
Lorsque le désir est plus large que le cœur
Et le plaisir plus rude et plus fort que la vie...

Pain and joy, boon friends, travel hand in hand.
My soul, like a savanna, lion-paced,
Pounds to the fierce beat of a grassy land...
Tempest and azure sky leave me their taste.

And oh, the ecstasy, vigor unbending,
Burning, to die one night still yearning-rife,
When, more vast than the heart, looms lust, unending,
And pleasure, stronger and more harsh than life...

"IL FERA LONGTEMPS CLAIR CE SOIR..."

Il fera longtemps clair ce soir, les jours allongent,
La rumeur du jour vif se disperse et s'enfuit,
Et les arbres, surpris de ne pas voir la nuit,
Demeurent éveillés dans le soir blanc, et songent...

Les marronniers, sur l'air plein d'or et de lourdeur,
Répandent leurs parfums et semblent les étendre;
On n'ose pas marcher ni remuer l'air tendre
De peur de déranger le sommeil des odeurs.

De lointains roulements arrivent de la ville...
La poussière, qu'un peu de brise soulevait,
Quittant l'arbre mouvant et las qu'elle revêt,
Redescend doucement sur les chemins tranquilles.

Nous avons tous les jours l'habitude de voir
Cette route si simple et si souvent suivie,
Et pourtant quelque chose est changé dans la vie,
Nous n'aurons plus jamais notre âme de ce soir...

“THE DAYS GROW LONG...”

The days grow long: this evening’s light will gleam
Into the shade; day’s murmur flitters, flees...
Wakeful, beneath a pallid sky, the trees
Wonder what has become of night, and dream...

The chestnuts strew their scents, heavy and deep,
Over the evening’s golden breath; we dare
Not take a step, nor stir the tender air,
Lest we arouse the perfumes from their sleep.

The echoes rumble from the far-off town;
A weary tree shakes loose its cloak of dust,
That rises, wafted on a gentle gust,
Over the tranquil paths, and settles down.

Daily we saw this road laid out before
Our eyes, traveled its calm simplicity;
But life, tonight, is changed somehow, and we
Have lost this evening’s soul forevermore...

L'IMAGE

Pauvre faune qui vas mourir,
Reflète-moi dans tes prunelles
Et fais danser mon souvenir
Entre les ombres éternelles.

Va, et dis à ces morts pensifs,
À qui mes jeux auraient su plaire,
Que je rêve d'eux sous les ifs
Où je passe petite et claire.

Tu leur diras l'air de mon front
Et ses bandelettes de laine,
Ma bouche étroite et mes doigts ronds
Qui sentent l'herbe et le troène.

Tu diras mes gestes légers
Qui se déplacent comme l'ombre
Que balancent dans les vergers
Les feuilles vives et sans nombre.

Tu leur diras que j'ai souvent
Les paupières lasses et lentes,
Qu'au soir je danse et que le vent
Dérange ma robe traînante.

Tu leur diras que je m'endors
Mes bras nus pliés sous ma tête,
Que ma chair est comme de l'or
Autour des veines violettes.

– Dis-leur comme ils sont doux à voir
Mes cheveux bleus comme des prunes,
Mes pieds pareils à des miroirs
Et mes deux yeux couleur de lune,

THE IMAGE

Poor fawn about to die, pray let
Me, by your eyes, reflected be,
And let the image of me yet
Dance amid shades, eternally.

Go, tell those pensive dead—those who
Enjoyed my pastimes pert—that, when
Brightly I pass beneath the yew,
I dream of them again... again...

Describe my brow, bound roundabout
With bands of woolen filigree;
My purse-lipped mouth, my fingers stout
That smell of grass and shrubbery.

Describe my sprightly gestures, soft
As shadows playing on the trees,
Lightly swaying the leaves aloft:
Myriad orchard energies...

Describe my heavy-lidded glance;
And how, oft-times, in flounces girt—
When, in the evening, I would dance—
The breeze jostles and swirls my skirt.

Describe how, as I sleep, I hold
My bare arms tucked beneath my head,
And how my skin, tinted with gold,
Sets off my veins deep-violeted.

—Tell them how lovely is my hair,
Plum-blue, that softly, sweetly lies;
And how my feet are like a pair
Of mirrors; and moonbeams, my eyes.

Et dis-leur que dans les soirs lourds,
Couchée au bord frais des fontaines,
J'eus le désir de leurs amours
Et j'ai pressé leurs ombres vaines...

And tell them how, on humid nights,
At eventide, by cool brook lying,
I lusted for their love's delights,
Caressed their empty shades, dead, dying...

LES ANIMAUX

Dieux gardiens des troupeaux qui tenez des houlettes,
Rendez-nous l'innocence ancestrale des bêtes;

Afin que nous ayons l'endurance des maux,
Donnez-nous la douceur des sobres animaux.

– Faites que nous ayons dans nos peines insignes
L'isolement muet et le dédain des cygnes;

Donnez-nous, pour souffrir le destin hasardeux,
L'indolence soumise et distraite des bœufs;

Faites que notre cœur où l'enfance se fane
Ait la gaîté robuste et la candeur de l'âne;

Donnez-nous, pour lutter contre les serments faux,
La défiance adroite et vive des oiseaux;

Faites que nous ayons, pour honorer nos veilles,
L'activité joyeuse et grave des abeilles;

Donnez-nous, pour calmer nos désirs et nos goûts,
L'insensibilité profonde des hiboux;

Et, dans les jours cruels où la raison divague,
Le calme des poissons arrêtés sur les vagues!

Faites que nous gardions le sens mystérieux
De l'infini qui dort dans le fond de leurs yeux,

– Et délivrez nos corps, misérables en somme,
De l'âme glorieuse et maudite de l'homme!...

THE ANIMALS

Crook-wielding gods who guard the flocks, give us
Beasts' age-old innocence ingenuous;

That we might have the strength our ills to bear,
Grant us the animals' poised, placid air;

—Bestow on us, in our consummate pain,
The lone swan's noble mien of mute disdain;

Give us, to brook fate's hazardous condition,
The oxen's indolent, bemused submission;

Let our heart, whose child-years fast slip away,
Enjoy the asses' joyous naiveté;

Give us, to parry false, sly eloquence,
The birds' defiance and their spry defense;

Let us, to fete night's honest gaieties,
Mimic the sober frolic of the bees;

Give us, to quell our lusty tastes and moods,
The owls' profound, impassive attitudes,

And, in distress, when reason misbehaves,
That resigned calm of fish caught on the waves!

Let us keep that infinite sense that lies
Asleep, deep in the mystery of their eyes,

—And free of our vulgar flesh, as best you can,
From the accursed—yet glorious—soul of man!...

LA MORT DIT Ā L'HOMME...

Voici que vous avez assez souffert, pauvre homme,
Assez connu l'amour, le désir, le dégoût,
L'âpreté du vouloir et la torpeur du somme,
L'orgueil d'être vivant et de pleurer debout...

Que voulez-vous savoir qui soit plus délectable
Que la douceur des jours que vous avez tenus?
Quittez le temps, quittez la maison et la table;
Vous serez sans regret ni peur d'être venu.

J'emplirai votre cœur, vos mains et votre bouche
D'un repos si profond, si chaud et si pesant,
Que le soleil, la pluie et l'orage farouche
Ne réveilleront pas votre âme et votre sang.

– Pauvre âme, comme au jour où vous n'étiez pas née,
Vous serez pleine d'ombre et de plaisant oubli.
D'autres iront alors par les rudes journées
Pleurant aux creux des mains, des tombes et des lits.

D'autres iront en proie au douloureux vertige
Des profondes amours et du destin amer,
Et vous serez alors la sève dans les tiges,
La rose du rosier et le sel de la mer.

D'autres iront blessés de désir et de rêve
Et leurs gestes feront de la douleur dans l'air,
Mais vous ne saurez pas que le matin se lève,
Qu'il faut revivre encore, qu'il fait jour, qu'il fait clair.

Ils iront retenant leur âme qui chancelle
Et trébuchant ainsi qu'un homme pris de vin;
– Et vous serez alors dans ma nuit éternelle,
Dans ma calme maison, dans mon jardin divin...

DEATH SAID TO MAN...

Now have you suffered quite enough, poor thing,
Known enough of desire, disgust, and love,
Of bitter wishing and sleep's mouldering,
Enough of living and the tears thereof...

What can you hope to know more tasteful yet
Than the sweetness of days that have been yours?
Leave time and table; go, without regret
Or fear for having come... Leave! Shut the doors.

And I shall fill your heart, mouth, hands with warm,
Wakeless repose, so heavy and so deep
That never sun, nor rain, nor savage storm
Will rouse your soul, your blood, out of their sleep.

–Poor thing! As on the day before your birth,
Yours, only thoughtless void and shadow-gloom;
Others will roam woe's days over the earth,
Shedding tears in their hands, their bed, their tomb.

Others will roam, prey to the dizzying grief
Of deep-felt loves and bitterest destiny;
And you, sap sweet, will flow through stem and leaf,
Rose growing on the bush, salt in the sea.

Others will roam and will their dream-wounds bear,
Wounds of desire, with gestures, empty, vain.
But you will not sense morning, unaware
That day dawns bright, that one must live again.

They will roam, holding back their stumbling soul,
Tottering like a man too drunk with wine;
–You will lie in my endless night's dark dole,
My peaceful mansion, my garden divine...

CHANSON DU TEMPS OPPORTUN

Le Temps, de ses pipeaux, tire de clairs accords:
Bondissez au soleil, les âmes et les corps;

Par les chemins poudreux et la verdure épaisse
Épuisez les plaisirs, c'est la seule sagesse;

Prenez-vous, quittez-vous, cherchez-vous tour à tour,
Il n'est rien de réel que le rêve et l'amour.

Sur la terre indigente où tant d'ombre s'éploie
Ayez souci d'un peu de justice et de joie;

Retenez, du savoir, ce qu'il faut au bonheur;
On est assez profond pour le jour où l'on meurt.

Vivez; ayez l'amour, la colère et l'envie,
Pauvres êtres vivants, il n'est rien que la vie!

SONG OF THE PROPER TIME

Time pipes its chords: and you, bodies and souls,
Leap, in the sun, your lusty caprioles!

On dusty path, in verdure lush and dense,
Wring delights dry: life has no other sense;

Take lovers, leave them, look for more thereof:
Nothing in life is real but dreams and love.

In poor earth's shadows, spread in ample measure,
Seek out a bit of justice and of pleasure.

Learn only joy's demands; for, by and by,
Wise enough will we be the day we die.

Live! Keep your love, your wrath, your eagerness,
Poor humans: life is all that you possess!

LA TERRE

Vous en qui le sommeil du monde est enfermé,
Terre de bon repos et de longues délices,
Dont le cœur ténébreux et rude est parfumé
Par les cèdres profonds et la douce réglisse,
Vous êtes l'urne auguste où les temps sont groupés;
La Nature sur vous se balance et s'égoutte
Comme un feuillage épais que la pluie a trempé
Et qui laisse pleuvoir son onde sur la route...
– Les abeilles des champs doriens, les étés,
La jeunesse odorante et chaude de la terre,
Les bois où les bergers de l'Hellas ont chanté,
Les plaisirs et les jours, c'est vous, sainte poussière!
C'est vous toute la gloire et tout l'amour humains:
Le corps d'Iphigénie et le coeur de Virgile
Et Chloé qui tenait des roses dans ses mains
Ont mêlé leur substance ardente à votre argile.
Vous êtes un autel rustique, où s'accomplit
Tout le mystérieux et fixe destin: l'homme
Vous apporte son cœur quand il l'a bien empli,
La mer son coquillage et le sapin sa gomme.
– Voici le champ fertile où l'humanité dort,
La couche aux plis profonds où tout entre et repose,
Le nocturne jardin où les houilles et l'or
Accueillent la venue éternelle des choses.
Tous ceux qui sous le ciel léger ont enseigné
La volupté riante et la bonne science,
Ont connu vos tombeaux et les ont imprégnés
D'une minutieuse et parfaite alliance.
C'est vous tous les désirs, c'est vous tous les efforts,
La corbeille où les fruits du lourd automne roulent,
La place populeuse où se pressent les morts,
C'est vous le pays large et sûr, c'est vous la foule!...

THE EARTH

O Earth, who worldly sleep enclose, in whom
Lies calm repose and glabrous permanence;
You whose rough heart, shadowed in darkling gloom,
Smells of deep cedars' licorice redolence;
You are the urn august, time-ashes' tomb.
Nature hovers above you, seeps her load
Of waters, falling drop by drop, intense,
Like rain-soaked foliage dripping on the road...
—Bees in the Doric fields, the succulence
Of summers, warm land's fragrant youth, sweet wood
Where sang the Hellene shepherd-innocents...
Pleasures, days... You, the soil of saintlihood!
You, human love and human glory sung:
Virgil's heart and Iphigenia's flesh,
And Chloe with rose handfuls strewn among
Your dust, and that passionately would enmesh
Their lust amid your clay... You are a shrine,
A rustic altar where man's destiny
Plays out, fixed in its mystery's design.
To you it is man brings his heart when he
Has filled it full; to you the sea will come
Bringing her shells; the evergreen, her gum.
—You, fertile field wherein humanity
Lies sleeping, you, couch furrowed deep, and where
All comes to rest; garden nocturnal, whose
Coal-blacks and golds bid endless welcome there
To everything's eternal rendezvous;
All who have spread beneath the lightsome skies
The happy knowledge of voluptuous bliss
Have known your tombs, and have, in minute wise,
Spawned, ample-sired, the perfect synthesis.
You, all desirings and all strivings; you,
The heavy cornucopia whence fall
Autumn's fair fruits; space vast and sure, whereto
The dead, pressed tight, come rest for good and all!

– Mon cœur plein de raison, et plein d'orgueil humain,
Nous aussi nous irons vers ces frères sans nombre,
Et je vous porterai devant moi, dans mes mains,
Pour que votre chaleur éclaire toute l'ombre…

—Proud, reasoned heart of mine! Soon, like the others,
We too shall venture to those teeming lands;
And I will hold you and reach forth my hands
To let your heat brighten my shadowed brothers...

Lines 14-15: The poet seems to be making an obliquely specific reference to the impending sacrifice of Iphigenia, daughter of Agamemnon and Clytemnestra, from which she was rescued by Artemis, as recounted by Euripides, Lucretius, Virgil, et al. The allusion to Chloé is more general, painting her merely as the prototypic shepherdess. Noailles will refer to her celebrated love affair with the shepherd Daphnis in *L'Honneur de souffrir* (see "Ni l'éblouissement du regard...," p. 196-97). (Trans.)

L'OMBRE DES JOURS

(1902)

LES VAGUES

Ô petites vagues frisées,
Qui vîtes, dans des temps si beaux,
D'entre les écumes des eaux
Surgir Aphrodite irisée,

Que ce jour soit comme un îlot
Qu'entoure votre âcre abondance,
Que chacun de mes désirs danse
Comme un rayon blanc sur le flot!

Voici que l'onde calme arrive
Et vient remuer le gravier
Où va plier et dévier
Sa perleuse et douce salive;

C'est comme si des doigts tremblants
Dérangeaient l'ordre de la grève,
Quand l'eau s'abaisse et se relève
En entraînant les cailloux blancs;

Allant et venant sur la pente,
Tous ces luisants cailloux roulés
Font un bruit de petites clés
Sous la molle écume fondante;

La terre et l'eau se mélangeant
Semblent unir deux lèvres claires;
J'ai soif de cette vague amère
En robe d'azur et d'argent.

– Vous savez bien, chère eau vivante,
Qu'il n'est d'amour si malaisé
Qui n'ait le désir du baiser,
De sa tendre et chaude épouvante;

THE WAVES

O little curling waves, whose eyes
Once saw—in finer, fairer days—
Up from the water's frothy haze,
A rainbowed Aphrodite rise,

May those days like an island be
Midst your brine's harsh luxuriance;
May each one of my wishes dance
Like a white ray about the sea!

Lo! how the water, calm, unfurls
Gently over the graveled shore,
Where—turning, twisting evermore—
It rolls its little spittle pearls;

It's as if trembling finger-play—
As rise and fall the waters—can
Disrupt the beach's ordered plan,
Whisking the pebbles, white, away;

Fro and to on the sloping swath,
A-roll, these pebbles, gleamingly
Sound like many a tinkling key
Beneath the softly frittering froth;

Water and land unite, like two
Bright lips joining as one; and I
Thirst for those waves that, bitter, ply
The shore in gown of silver-blue.

You know, O waters flowing free,
That love, however brash, is driven
By the wish that a kiss be given,
Tenderly fearsome though it be.

Vous savez que rien n'est si fort
Que la caresse et que l'étreinte,
Et que toute tendresse est feinte
Qui n'a le vouloir de l'accord.

C'est pourquoi, mes vagues ailées,
Ce matin, dans le sable doux,
Je me mettrai sur mes genoux
Et je boirai votre eau salée...

You know one plights no stronger troth
Than with embraces' true caress,
And that false is the tenderness
That is not deep-desired by both.

And that is why, winged wavelets mine,
This morning, on the gentle sand,
I shall kneel down before you, and
There shall my lips sip deep your brine...

Line 4: The reference is, no doubt, to Botticelli's famous 1486 painting *The Birth of Venus.* (Trans.)

LES OMBRES

Quand, ayant beaucoup travaillé,
J'aurai, le cœur de pleurs mouillé,
Cessé de vivre,
J'irai voir le pays où sont
Tous les bons faiseurs de chansons
Avec leur livre.

– Chère ombre de François Villon
Qui, comme un grillon au sillon,
Te fis entendre,
Que n'ai-je pu presser tes mains
Quand on voulait sur les chemins
Te faire pendre!

Verlaine qui vas titubant,
Chantant et semblable au dieu Pan
Aux pieds de laine,
Es-tu toujours simple et divin,
Ivre de ferveur et de vin,
Bon saint Verlaine?

Et vous dont le destin fut tel
Qu'il n'en est pas de plus cruel,
Pauvre Henri Heine,
Ni de plus beau chez les humains,
Mettez votre front dans mes mains,
Pensons à peine.

Moi, par la vie et ses douleurs,
J'ai goûté l'ardeur et les pleurs
Plus qu'on ne l'ose...
Laissez que, lasse, près de vous,
Ô mes dieux si sages et fous
Je me repose...

THE SHADES

When I put all my labors by,
Once done, and when, heart-tearful, I
Have ceased to be,
I'll visit, in my wandering,
That land where the fine songsters sing
Their poetry.

–Dear Villon's shade, who, like the cricket
Chirping his song in furrow-thicket,
Sang clear your cry,
Why could I not press tight your hand
Once they, over the highroad, planned
To hang you high!

Verlaine, poor tottering drunkard-man
Who sang like the wool-footed Pan,
God-denizen
Divine! Still naïve, drunk are you,
As then, on wine and passion too,
Dear Saint Verlaine?

And you, poor Heine, desolate,
Disconsolate... Cruelest your fate,
You, sad distraught,
Fairest of men, be comforted:
Here in my hands come lay your head,
With never a thought.

Myself, wearied by life, I know
The taste of burning tears and woe
More than is best...
O gods–mad, wise–I pray you yet
Suffer me by your side, and let
Me take my rest...

Line 19: The rhyme in the original preserves the French pronunciation of the German poet Heine's name, unfamiliar to Anglo-Saxon–or even German–ears. (Trans.)

ATTENDRISSEMENT

Maison où j'ai passé tous les plus tendres mois
De mon aventureuse et frissonnante vie,
Mon rêve vous bâtit dans mon âme ravie,
Et voici qu'aujourd'hui je vous habite en moi!

Je revois les moments oppressés du voyage,
Où, quittant la cité pour votre plus doux air,
Je demeurais, la nuit, grave et les yeux ouverts,
Toute roulée au beau désir de votre image.

Ô porte du jardin qui grince sur ses gonds
Et s'écarte en chassant des graviers autour d'elle,
Cependant qu'apparaît, plein de lys et d'ombelles,
Le verger vert, avec son odeur d'estragon!

– La maison! son vitrail léger comme des bulles
D'eau transparente où joue un vif soleil tremblant,
Le dallage, alterné de marbre noir et blanc,
L'écho et la senteur de bois du vestibule!

Et puis la pièce basse où l'on entrait d'abord,
La terrasse avec deux tonneaux de porcelaine,
Le jardin, son gazon et ses corbeilles pleines
D'une sauge velue et bleue, qui sentait fort.

Les chambres: de naïfs papiers aux murs s'élancent,
Papiers de fleurs, d'oiseaux, de personnages clairs,
Papiers simples et doux, qui répètent leurs airs
Comme une monotone et sensible romance.

Tout le matin c'était la fête du dieu Pan,
Et puis venait le soir, l'heure où l'âme s'ennuie,
Et songe et se désole, et parfois à la pluie
On entendait crier et s'effrayer les paons.

TENDERNESS

House where I spent the gentlest months I knew
Of all my throbbing life adventuresome...
Dream-built within my soul, here have you come
Today, to live in me and I in you.

I see again moments of travel—drear,
Oppressive—when, for your sweet air I lay,
Eyes open and longing the night away,
Enwrapped in yearning to see you appear.

O grating garden-gate, opening on
The orchard green, sweeping the graveled ground
Where lilies' petal-parasols abound,
Heavy with the perfume of tarragon.

The house! And light as bubbles clear, where stood,
Trembling, the sun at play; the window bright
Of hue; the floor-tiles, marble, black and white;
The hallway's echo and its scent of wood!

Then, stepping down, the terrace one passed through...
The garden with two porcelain urns, the lawn,
The baskets heaped with sage, set out upon
The grass, and pungent in their downy blue.

The bedrooms; walls papered in sentiment's
Naïve motifs; papers with debonair
Figures—birds, flowers—repeating the same air
Like heartfelt song, dull in its innocence.

Mornings, one feted Pan, outside and in;
But evening fell on boredom's blear domain
Of dream-laments; and sometimes, come the rain,
One heard the peacocks raise their frightful din.

L'héliotrope mauve aux senteurs de vanille
Emplissait l'air penchant d'évanouissement;
Au coup de vent du soir on voyait par moment
L'eau du bassin s'enfler en forme de coquille;

Et quand la nuit d'argent et de fusain venait,
Toute lisse, avec, au milieu, sa lune ronde,
Les arbres allégés, les collines et l'onde
Prenaient un délicat et sombre air japonais.

– Rien n'est changé là-bas, mais j'ai changé moi-même.
Ce n'est plus qu'en rêvant que je revois encor
Ces beaux soleils, venus de l'âme et du dehors,
Près de qui, comme un flot d'abeilles qui essaiment,
Mon plaisir tournoyait avec des ailes d'or!...

Mauve heliotrope spread its vanilla smell
About, fainting, head bowed... An evening breeze
Might swell the billows of the pond, and these
Would well up, bulging like a cockleshell.

And when night, charcoal-silvered, took its ease–
Smooth-skied, with full round moon amidst, now light
And graceful grown–the hills, the water might
Look darkly, delicately Japanese...

Nothing has changed there. Nothing. Only I
Have changed... No more in dreams' imaginings
I see suns born of soul, of air. Fair things
About which, like a swarm of bees, would fly,
A-swirl, my pleasure on its golden wings!...

ÉMERVEILLEMENT

Mon Dieu, je ne puis pas dire combien est fort
Mon cœur de ce matin devant le soleil d'or,
Devant tout ce qui brille et scintille dehors.

Faudra-t-il que jamais je n'épuise ma joie
De cette eau qui reluit, de cet air qui me noie,
De tout ce qui du temps en mon âme poudroie!

Viendront-elles un jour, en quelque paradis,
Ces collines pour qui j'ai tant fait et tant dit,
M'apporter la chaleur du parfum de midi?

Sera-ce ma naïve et belle récompense
Que les arbres, avec leurs branches qui s'avancent,
Me présentent des fleurs pleines de complaisance?

Entendrai-je le fin et patient remous
Des râteaux de l'été passant dans les cailloux
Comme des mains qui font un travail long et doux?

Aurai-je des maisons aux toits de tuiles roses,
Avec du ciel autour, qui glisse et se repose
Sur les jardins, sur les chemins, sur toutes choses?...

Verrai-je, quand le jour jaune va se levant,
Sur les routes, au bord du mur blanc d'un couvent,
Passer des chariots avec des bœufs devant,

Et verrai-je un village heureux, avec sa foule
Des dimanches, flânant, et ses ruisseaux qui coulent
Près des enclos plantés de chanvre et de ciboules?

Pourrai-je en respirant goûter l'odeur du temps,
Et me faire le cœur si tendre et si cédant,
Que les oiseaux de l'air viendront loger dedans?

WONDER AND AWE

Dear God, my heart is stronger than I dare
Profess; that heart, strong in the sun-gold air,
Sparkling on everything and everywhere.

Must my joy last unspent and endless; must
I prize each shimmering wave, each drowning gust,
All that, within my soul, turns to time's dust!

Those hills... Off in some paradise, will they,
Who offered me so much to do and say,
Blow me the perfumed heat born of midday?

Will the trees–ample limbs outstretched–collude
To strew on me in generous, artless mood,
The flower tokens of their gratitude?

Will I hear that unhurried give-and-take
Of pebbles grated by the summer rake,
Like hands laboring long for sweet chores' sake?

Will I have houses, roofs in pink tiles dressed,
And sky gliding astride, settling to nest
Over the gardens, paths, and all the rest?

Will I see–when dawn's gold is on the rise–
Beside white convent wall, before my eyes,
Carts plodding down the road, drawn oxen-wise?

And will I see a happy village thrive;
Lazing in Sunday throng; gutters alive
That stream past garden-plots of hemp and chive?

Will time's taste fragrance-fill my breath, and bring
My heart a tenderness so welcoming
That nestling birds repose beneath its wing?

– Ô petite, divine, auguste et grande terre,
Place des jeux, place des jours et du mystère,
Puisque l'humain désir en vous se désaltère,

Pourquoi faut-il que moi je n'aie jamais cela,
Ce bon apaisement du corps content et las,
Et que toujours mon cœur vers vous vole en éclats?...

–O earth! Small, great, steeped in divinity,
Source of days' pleasures, of days' mystery...
Since you slake man's desires, why must I be

Ever denied that peace, that blandishment
Of happiness you grant to flesh outspent,
Yearning, to my heart's bursting discontent?...

LE CONSEIL

Va, sois peureuse du destin:
Ce qui n'était pas ce matin
Viendra ce soir comme une flèche,
Dans le désir que rien n'empêche...
Le lendemain n'est pas tracé:
Tu n'es sûre que du passé.
Il est à toi, tu peux le prendre;
Mais, dans l'ombre qui va descendre,
Rien du hasard ne t'est connu;
Je sens comme ton cœur est nu,
Tendre, brûlant et taciturne;
Ne crains-tu pas Vénus nocturne,
Et les atteintes de l'Amour
Qui vient hardiment, à son jour,
Menant l'étincelant vacarme?
Ah! tant de plaisirs et de larmes...

ADVICE

Ah, madame, fear your destiny:
What today's morn brings not will be
Winging its way, shot like a dart
Tonight, to pierce the very heart
Of your desire... Without a doubt,
Tomorrows are not yet traced out.
The past is yours alone to keep,
Changeless and sure; but fate, clad deep
In shadow, hides its face. I sense
Your tender heart laid low–intense,
Taciturn... What? Do you not fear
Venus by night? Or Love, who here
Presses his brash attack with his
Brawling troop, when his day it is
To lead his pack: days all or any!
Yes, tears and pleasures... Ah, so many...

LA QUERELLE

Va-t'en, je ne veux plus regarder ton regard,
Voir tes yeux plus lointains et plus doux que la nue,
Ta joue où les rayons du jour d'or sont épars,
Ta bouche qui sourit et qui ment, ta main nue...

Va-t'en, éloigne-toi de mon désir ce soir,
Tout de toi me ravit, m'irrite et me tourmente.
Loin de tes bras, trompeurs et chers, je vais m'asseoir
Dans la plaine assoupie où se bercent les menthes.

Et là, oubliant tout du mal que tu me fais,
J'entendrai, les yeux clos, l'esprit las, le cœur sage,
Sous les hêtres d'argent pleins d'ombre et de reflets,
La respiration paisible du feuillage...

THE QUARREL

Go! I no longer want to see that glance
You glance at me, softer than cloud-mist, and
More distant; or your cheek, where sun's rays dance
Their gold; your mouth, false, smiling; or your hand...

Go! Flee my evening passion, let me be,
You who are all my bliss, ennui, and woe.
Far from your dear, deceiving arms, let me
Doze where the mint goes swaying, to and fro.

Forgetting all your hurtfulness, content
In silvered beeches' glinting shades, eyes closing,
I shall give ear, heart wise but spirit spent,
To the calm breathing of their leaves reposing...

LA POURSUITE

Les cœurs voudraient bien se connaître,
Mais l'Amour danse entre les êtres,
Il va de l'une à l'autre attente
Et, comme le vent fait aux plantes,
Il mêle les douces essences;
Mais les âmes qui se distancent
Sont plus rapides dans leur course
Que l' air, le parfum et la source
Et cherchent en vain à se prendre.
L'amour n'est ni joyeux ni tendre...

THE CHASE

Hearts yearn to know each other, yet
Love does its little minuet
Amongst them, now between, betwixt,
Full of its lush aromas, mixed,
As when the wind goes blowing on
The plants; but souls are quickly gone,
Fleeing, more rapid in their going
Than air, perfume, or river flowing:
Each would, in vain, its mate possess.
Love knows nor joy nor tenderness...

LES REGRETS

Allez, je veux rester seule avec les tombeaux;
– Les morts sont sous la terre et le matin est beau,
L'air a l'odeur de l'eau, de l'herbe, du feuillage,
Les morts sont dans la mort pour le reste de l'âge...
Un jour, mon corps dansant sera semblable à eux,
J'aurai l'air de leur front, le vide de leurs yeux,
J'accomplirai cet acte unique et solitaire,
Moi qui n'ai pas dormi seule, aux jours de la terre!
– Tout ce qui doit mourir, tout ce qui doit cesser,
La bouche, le regard, le désir, le baiser!
Être la chose d'ombre et l'être de silence
Tandis que le printemps vert et vermeil s'élance
Et monte trempé d'or, de sève et de moiteur!
Avoir eu comme moi le cœur si doux, le cœur
Plein de plaisir, d'espoir, de rêve et de mollesse
Et ne plus s'attendrir de ce que l'aube naisse;
Être au fond du repos l'éternité du temps...
– D'autres seront alors vivants, joyeux, contents.
Des hommes marcheront auprès des jeunes filles,
Ils verront des labours, des moissons, des faucilles,
La couleur délicate et changeante des mois.
Moi, je ne verrai plus, je serai morte, moi,
Je ne saurai plus rien de la douceur de vivre...
Mais ceux-là qui liront les pages de mon livre,
Sachant ce que mon âme et mes yeux ont été,
Vers mon ombre riante et pleine de clarté
Viendront, le cœur blessé de langueur et d'envie,
Car ma cendre sera plus chaude que leur vie...

REGRETS

I want to stay among the tombs, alone;
–The dead lie buried under every stone,
Dwelling in death for all eternity...
The smell of water, grasses, greenery,
Rise at fair dawn and hang upon the air.
Like them, I shall one day be dwelling there,
My dancing body, stilled, my brow, a shell
Like theirs; and empty-orbed, my eyes as well.
I shall do what, my whole life, I did not:
To sleep alone, at last, will be my lot!
–All that must cease to be, all that must die:
Glances, desires, lips, kisses... Gone! And I
Will lie, a silent shade, a shadow mute,
Though spring–green, ruddy–bursts forth resolute
And, drenched in gold and sap, rises aloft!
To think that I once had a heart so soft,
So filled with pleasures, dreams, and hopes, and yet
Hunger no more for what dawn might beget;
To be eternity, deep, timeless... Then
Others will live, joyous, content; and men
Will saunter with their maidens, witnessing
The plantings and the scythes at harvesting,
The months changing their colors tenderly.
None of this I myself, now dead, shall see,
Nor shall I know life's sweetness... But in ages
Yet to come, those whose eyes peruse my pages,
Knowing what my eyes and my soul had been,
Will sense my laughing shadow, crystalline,
Heart-sore they, and with anguished envy rife,
For better still my ashes than their life...

“J’ÉCRIS POUR QUE LE JOUR…”

J’écris pour que le jour où je ne serai plus
On sache comme l’air et le plaisir m’ont plu,
Et que mon livre porte à la foule future
Comme j’aimais la vie et l’heureuse Nature.

Attentive aux travaux des champs et des maisons,
J’ai marqué chaque jour la forme des saisons,
Parce que l’eau, la terre et la montante flamme
En nul endroit ne sont si belles qu’en mon âme!

J’ai dit ce que j’ai vu et ce que j’ai senti,
D’un cœur pour qui le vrai ne fut point trop hardi,
Et j’ai eu cette ardeur, par l’amour intimée,
Pour être, après la mort, parfois encore aimée,

Et qu’un jeune homme, alors, lisant ce que j’écris,
Sentant par moi son cœur ému, troublé, surpris,
Ayant tout oublié des épouses réelles,
M’accueille dans son âme et me préfère à elles…

"I WRITE SO THAT, WHEN I NO MORE SHALL BE..."

I write so that, when I no more shall be,
One sees how air and pleasure pleasured me;
That love of life and Nature fill my pages
Before the myriad eyes of future ages.

Keen to the task of field and household chore,
I sang each day the season marked therefor,
Because earth, water, flame–all I extol–
Are nowhere near as fair as in my soul!

Everything that I saw and felt I told,
Nor did my heart esteem the truth too bold;
And, love-inspired, I breathed my ardent breath
Hoping that I be loved yet after death,

And that some young man, reading what I've written,
Feeling his heart surprised and passion-smitten,
Will wives of flesh and blood cast from his head,
And welcome me into his soul instead...

“VOUS QUE JAMAIS RIEN NE DÉLIE...”

Vous que jamais rien ne délie,
Ô ma pauvre âme dans mon corps,
Pourrez-vous, ma mélancolie,
Ayant bu le vin et la lie,
Connaître la bonne folie
De l'éternel repos des morts?

– Vous si vivace et si profonde,
Âme de rêve et de transport,
Qui, pareille à la terre ronde
Portez tous les désirs du monde,
Buveuse de l'air et de l'onde,
Pourrez-vous entrer dans ce port?

Dans le port de calme sagesse,
De ténèbres et de sommeil,
Où ni l'amour ni la détresse
N'étirent la tiède paresse,
Et ne font, – mon âme faunesse, –
Siffler les flèches du soleil!...

“O MELANCHOLIC SOUL OF MINE...”

O melancholic soul of mine!
Poor soul, ever a part of me,
Will you, once you have drunk the wine
Down to the dregs, seize the design
Of endless rest, folly benign:
Death, life’s eternal destiny?

–You, sage so spry, so debonair,
O soul of bliss, of reverie,
Who all the weighty passions bear
Of earthly sphere; do you bid fair,
You, who glut, gorge on sea and air,
To enter that port willingly?

That port of wisdom’s restfulness,
Of shades and sleep’s oblivion,
Where neither love nor life’s duress
Tug at the calm–mild, motionless–
Or–O my soul, my satyress!–
Cast whistling darts down from the sun!...

LES ÉBLOUISSEMENTS

(1907)

ÉBLOUISSEMENT

Quelquefois, dans la nuit, on s'éveille en sursaut,
Et, comme un choc qui brise et qui perce les os,
On songe au temps qui fuit, aux plus jeunes années,
À. l'aurore enflammant les vitres fortunées,
Aux fougueux papillons qui, sur la paix des blés,
Se poursuivaient pareils à des jasmins ailés.
Les odorantes fleurs étaient des puits, des jattes;
Les abeilles dansaient autour des aromates,
Et leur vol chaud semblait aux plantes retenu
Par un fil lumineux, élastique et ténu;
Comme un clair groupement de forces bondissantes,
Les collines riaient, triomphantes, luisantes.
Jeunes jours dont l'accent ne peut pas revenir,
Qui nous consolera de tous nos souvenirs?
Ô matins de quinze ans, où le corps tendre et preste
S'alliait à l'arome, à la chaleur céleste,
Où les oiseaux montaient d'un vol facile et pur,
Où tout l'être semblait aspiré par l'azur,
Où l'on palpait l'odeur, l'air, l'horizon, les vagues,
Avec la main qui tremble et l'esprit qui divague!
Matins où l'on était solitaire et vainqueur,
Où l'on sentait courir les fleuves sur son cœur,
Où l'on goûtait, buvant l'aurore sur la cime,
La divine pudeur de se sentir sublime!
Où le désir, à l'aigle audacieux pareil,
Était un arc d'argent qui vise le soleil!
Pensif, l'on se sentait indispensable au monde;
L'on se disait: « Ma vie où le désir abonde,
Le flambeau de mes yeux, mon bras tendre et pressant
Rajeuniront demain l'univers languissant... »
Je me souviens des soirs en mai sur la terrasse:
L'odeur d'un oranger engourdissait l'espace,
Et je sentais, venant par tous les blancs chemins,
Le soir apprivoisé se coucher dans mes mains...
Sans pouvoir distinguer les formes, les visages,

THE DAZZLING

At times, by night, we wake up with a start,
A shock that seems to wrench our bones apart,
Dreaming of time's quick-fleeting flight, years gone,
Youth fled, and of a once new-flaming dawn
Shining on windows fine-arrayed, and eyes
That watched the to-and-fro of butterflies'
Frenetic chasings and meanderings
Skimming the peaceful grain like jasmine wings.
The fragrant blooms were wells, bowls; and the bees,
In the heat of their dancing revelries
About the spice-rich petals, would appear
Held to the flowers by a glistening, sheer
Elastic thread... The hills, a clustering troop
Of bounding energies, would chaff and whoop
Their triumph, gleaming... O youth, gone! Now still,
Forever and anon, your voice! Who will
Console me for our memories? And you,
Morns of our fifteen years, when bodies new
And fresh were steeped yet in the firmament's
Gentle warmth and the sweet celestial scents;
When birds, in pure, effortless flight, would rise
Aloft, and when it seemed the azured skies
Would draw us ever upward; and when we,
With trembling hand and in mind's fantasy,
Could hold and press the very air, the smells,
The far horizon, and the ocean swells.
Mornings when we, a conqueror solitary,
Could feel the rivers coursing through the very
Depths of our heart; when, drinking in dawn's light
As its first rays played on the summits' height,
We tasted chaste divinity untold!
When our desire, spanning like eagle bold,
Reached in a silvered arc seeking the sun.
Pensive, we knew the world would come undone
Without us: "With my life, with my desires,
My firm but tender strength, my eyes' torch-fires,
Tomorrow will the age-bowed world grow young..."
I recall terrace-nights in May, among

De tout je me disais: « C'est Eros qui voyage. »
Les ailes des oiseaux et les pas des passants
Faisaient un même bruit de désir dans mon sang.
Sous le magnolia, le cèdre, les troènes,
L'odeur coulait ainsi que de chaudes fontaines,
Et, l'âme épouvantée et le cœur éperdu,
Je demandais à l'infini: « Que me veux-tu? »
La lune, sur la mer mollement agitée,
Par chaque flot mouvant paraissait emportée,
Et, sous l'astre laiteux aux bondissants regards,
Toute la mer semblait blanche de nénuphars...
Je contemplais cette eau luisante, énigmatique.
Je me disais: « Là-bas, c'est la puissante Afrique,
C'est le cri des félins par l'écho répété,
C'est l'inimaginable et meurtrier été,
C'est la rage divine et l'écume de l'âme... »
Et j'étendais ma main pour toucher cette flamme.

– Aujourd'hui, le cœur las et blessé par le feu,
Je vous bénis encore, ô brasier jaune et bleu,
Exaltant univers dont chaque élan m'enivre!
Mourante, je dirai qu'il faut jouir et vivre;
Que, malgré la langueur d'un corps triste et brûlant,
La nuit est généreuse et le jour succulent;
Que les larmes, les cris, la douleur, l'agonie
Ne peuvent pas ternir l'allégresse infinie;
Qu'un moment du désir, qu'un moment de l'été
Contiennent la suave et chaude éternité.
Ô sol humide et noir d'où jaillit la jacinthe!
Qu'importe si dans l'âpre et ténébreuse enceinte
Les morts sont étendus froids et silencieux?
Ô beauté des tombeaux sous la douceur des cieux!
Marbres posés ainsi que des bornes plaintives,
Rochers mystérieux des incertaines rives,
Horizontale porte accédant à la nuit,
Ô débris du vaisseau; épave qui reluit,
Comme vous célébrez la joie et l'abondance,
La force du plaisir, l'audace de la danse,

An orange tree's perfumes, the space benumbing,
And I sensed, over the white pathways coming
Toward me, the evening, and I captured him,
Docile, holding him in my hands. Eyes dim
And mind perplexed, I told myself: "No doubt,
Eros it is, who goes gadding about."
Birds' flapping wings, man's pacings on the ground...
And in my blood the single pounding sound
Of my desiring, as, under the trees–
Magnolia, cedar, humble shrubberies–
Wafted a redolence like water flowing
Warm from a fountain; as my poor soul, growing
Desperate, heart-lost, I asked infinity:
"Tell me, what is it you would do with me?"
The waters' face, with every billow seeming
To spirit off the moon, milky-white beaming,
Appeared outspread with water-lilies round...
I watched that sparkling sea that would confound
And puzzle me. I told myself: "Out there
Is Africa, the powerful, whose air
Echoes the great cats' growling cries, whose lot
Is endless summer, murderous, hot, and not
To be believed... Soul-froth, heaven's wild ire..."
And I reached out my hand to touch that fire.

–Today, flame-seared, heart-weary, yet I bless
Your every leap, your every limitless
Striving, yearning, O blaze of gold and blue,
Burning me drunk with passion-fire for you!
Dying, I shall repeat that one must live
This life with all the strength one's flesh can give;
That, though the body languish, though it ache
And burn, still night is generous; day will break
Straightway, certain to strew its succulence,
Its ample store; that anguish's laments,
Moans, tears, no more in agony shall be
Sore spent to tarnish an infinity
Of happiness; that one moment's desire,
One moment flaming with the summer's fire
Holds all eternity's soft heat... O earth–

L'universelle arène aux lumineux gradins!
– Et quelquefois, parmi les funèbres jardins,
Je crois voir, ses pieds nus appuyés sur les tombes,
Un Eros souriant qui nourrit des colombes...

Humid, and rich, and black—whence springs to birth
The hyacinth! What matters it if, deep
Within the womb of bitter shadow, sleep
The dead, in chill and silent tomb! How fair,
You graves of heavenly beauty lying there
Beneath the sky, fine marbles, headstones placed
Like milestones, mourning; cliffs edging the waste
Along mysterious shores, vague to the view,
And sidewise doors unto the night... O you,
Wreck of the vessel, flotsam of the sea,
How joyous, how abundant your debris—
Energy measureless!—with celebrants
Bold in the boundless pleasure of the dance!
O world's arena bathed in glorious light!
—At times, to graveyard gardens come, I might
See, leaning on the tombs, a sight beguiling:
Feeding the doves, a barefoot Eros, smiling!...

SOIR D'ESPAGNE

Les verts camélias, sur la poudreuse route,
Ouvrent leurs blanches, roses fleurs,
Petits vases glacés dont nul miel ne s'égoutte
Malgré l'assiégeante chaleur.

Mais les pourpres œillets aux flammes ténébreuses
Aux pétales aigus, ardents,
Semblent déchiquetés par des mains amoureuses,
Par des ongles et par des dents;

Et leur suave odeur, leur émouvante extase
Saturent l'éther vif et mol;
La cloche sonne au toit du clocher de topaze...
Ô langueur d'un soir espagnol!

Dans la rue, un parfum de poisson cru s'exhale.
Assis sous un auvent de bois,
Un bel adolescent fabrique des sandales,
Insouciant comme les rois.

Sur le bord de la mer, où le sel bleu des vagues
Mord l'azur d'un cuisant éclat,
Une usine répand des parfums doux et vagues
De cannelle et de chocolat.

Et puis c'est le désert: une morne étendue
De fossés, de talus pelés.
La cathédrale énorme est dans l'air suspendue,
Couleur d'or, de sucre brûlé.

De petits enfants bruns, comme de sombres anges
Mêlent leurs corps déshabillés
Dans les ruisseaux étroits où roulent des oranges,
Près des boutiques des barbiers.

SPANISH EVENING

The green camellias, on the dusty road,
Open their pink-white blooms; each flower,
A glazed vase, drips none of its honey-load
Despite the heat's oppressive power.

Crimson carnations, somber-flamed, with pointed,
Burning-hued petals, seem to be
Bitten asunder, ripped apart, disjointed
By hands, but no less lovingly;

And their smooth fragrance svelte, their tremolo
Of bliss, soak soft the ether, light
Of touch... Bell tolls in topaz belfry... O
Languorous, languid, Spanish night!

Welling up from the street, a raw-fish scent...
Under a wooden covering,
A handsome lad sews sandals, as content
And carefree as a very king.

On the shore, where the salt-blue waves–intense,
Harsh–bite the azure, mild, dim-spun
Aromas spread a factory's redolence
Of chocolate and of cinnamon...

And then, the vast terrain, dismal and bare–
Ditches, bald clumps of earth; but bold,
Huge, the cathedral, hanging in the air,
The color of burnt-sugar gold...

Little brown children, angels tan of skin,
Frolicking by the barber shops,
Play naked in the gutter-streams wherein
Roll oranges and kitchen-slops.

– Ô misère animale, active, triomphante,
Ô saveur de la pauvreté,
Sous le ciel des guerriers, des trônes, des infantes,
Dans le brasier bleu de l'été!

Qu'importe à ces humains dont le cœur est farouche
La chétive privation?
Ils ont leurs corps dansants, leurs bras ambrés, leur bouche,
Ils ont la sainte passion!

Sur ces rocs désolés où l'Océan se brise,
Où le destin les relégua,
Ils respirent, la nuit, dans l'odeur de la brise;
Les beaux jardins de Malaga.

Ils ont la maison blanche et le balcon d'ébène,
Le piment épais et vermeil,
Et, pour les jeux sanglants, dans l'exaltante arène,
Des places d'ombre et de soleil.

Ils ont leur sombre église à leurs amours propice;
Dans ce royaume d'argent noir,
Dans les niches, couleur de résine et d'épice,
La Vierge luit comme un miroir.

Et l'amant torturé offre un cierge qui fume
À ce beau visage oppressé,
Et contemple, au travers de ces vapeurs d'écume,
Cette Vénus au sein percé,

Et, l'enlaçant soudain d'un tendre et triste geste,
Lui dit: « Ô ma plaintive sœur,
Quel rival enflammé de ton amant céleste
T'a mis ce couteau dans le cœur? »

—O bestial wretchedness, triumphant, thriving!
O poverty, savory and sweet...
Sky of infantas, warriors, thrones, surviving
In summertime's blue furnace-heat!

What of it? Base privation barely dims
The fevered hearts pounding a-fresh—
In dancing bodies, voices, amber limbs—
The sacred passion of the flesh!

On these bleak cliffs where breaks the Ocean, where
Destiny left them to their doom,
At night they breathe, borne on the breezes, fair
Malaga's garden-air perfume.

Theirs, the white house, the ebony balcony,
Hot peppers—thick, red... And, when one
Throbs to the bullring's bloody revelry,
Theirs, a seat in the shade or sun.

Theirs, the dark church, well-fit for their amours,
Where, in her silver-dusk domain,
Virgin, in resin-spice niche-miniatures,
Shines like a brilliant mirror-pane.

Lover tormented offers her icon—
She of the visage sore oppressed—
A candle; through the froth-mist, gazes on
This Venus of the heart-stabbed breast,

And, with a soulful and embracing glance,
Suddenly cries: "Poor sister mine,
Who pierced your heart? Whose wild exuberance
Rivaled your lover's love divine?"

JOUR D'ÉTÉ

Le matin lumineux semble une chaude neige,
Et luit comme un dessin qu'une vitre protège.
Nulle ombre ne ternit ce calme long, égal;
L'azur a l'éclat net et dur d'un minéral;
La verdure est d'un vert trop doux, plus doux encore...
À chaque arbre s'enroule une liquide aurore;
Un geai semble emporté vers la claire hauteur
Par la force et l'élan d'un battement de cœur!
Les fleurs, sur la pelouse où des agneaux vont paître,
Ont le rouge et le bleu d'une fête champêtre;
L'ombrage se déverse et fait de noirs étangs
Où l'insecte et l'oiseau se reposent, contents.
Douce diversité des feuilles et des lignes!
Sous les ormes luisants où s'agrafent les vignes
On croit voir s'élancer, au son du tympanon,
Les nymphes et les beaux garçons d'Anacréon!...
– Ô tendre flamboiement, l'immense gratitude
Pour tant de paix, de joie heureuse, d'altitude,
S'agite dans mon cœur comme un flot triomphant,
Comme des rameaux clairs portés par des enfants!
Les coteaux, dans le ciel léger, s'évanouissent
À force de chaleur, de vapeurs, de délices.
Une exaltation soulève l'Univers,
Les cieux, tranchants et vifs, pénètrent les bois verts,
Le mol pétunia, l' œillet, les chèvrefeuilles
Donnent leur goût divin aux brises qu'ils recueillent.
Luxurieuse ardeur du languissant été!
Les monts d'argent sont des soupirs de volupté;
Tout mon cœur vaporeux d'entre mes bras s'envole,
Je ris, je tends les mains, je baise l'herbe molle,
Et là-bas, dans l'azur, un train s'est enfoncé

SUMMER DAY

The morning glistens, like a warm snowshine,
And glitters like some glass-encased design.
No shadow dulls this long, smooth calm; a sheen
Glows on the azure, like a metal, clean
And hard; the foliage lies soft, too soft...
A liquid dawn surrounds each tree; aloft,
A jay seems swept up toward the sunlit height,
Borne on a heartbeat! In the meadows, bright,
Where sheep will graze, the blossoms, blue and red,
Look like a village fair; shadow-pools spread
Patches of darkness here and there, in which
Insect and bird, contented, find a niche,
To rest. Under the elms, where vines entwine–
Gentle diversity of leaf and line!–
Dreaming, one sees Anacreon's nymphs, beaus,
Reveling in the timbrel's tremolos!...
–O blaze of tenderness, my limitless
Thanks for this peace, these heights of happiness
Stirring my heart in floods of triumph, streaming,
Like boughs, fronds wafting in young hands, light, gleaming!
So much the heat, the haze, such the delight,
That hillocks in the sheer sky fade from sight.
The Universe wells up in ecstasy,
The heavens' sharp edge cuts through the greenery;
Pinks, woodbines, frail petunias, breeze-embraced,
Offer their gift divine of scent and taste.
Languorous, torrid, sumptuous summer day!
Distant, the hills and hummocks, silver-gray,
Are sighs of bliss; my heart melts, mist-like, flees
My grasp, goes soaring, and I laugh, and seize
The soft grass in my hands and kiss it, as
A train, whistling its cry of triumph, has

Avec son cri de joie et ses sanglots pressés,
Tandis que, détaché d'une invisible fronde,
Un doux oiseau jaillit jusqu'au sommet du monde!...

Gone lunging in the azure, off somewhere,
Gasping its breathy sobs, while, in the air,
A bird, loosed by a sling unseen, is hurled
Heavenward, to the summit of the world!...

Lines 15-16: In referring to Anacreon, the Greek lyric poet (ca 570-480 B.C.E.), the author most likely has in mind the love poems and drinking songs long incorrectly attributed to him, and to the imitations they inspired, since his own authenticated compositions are fragmentary and few in number. (Trans.)

POÈME DE L'AZUR

Le jour d'été suffoque, étouffe, perd haleine
Sous l'implacable ciel de blanche porcelaine.
Tout brûle, consumé d'un voile de safran,
Et rêve à quelque acide, invisible torrent...
Les souffles, les élans, les chants, les rumeurs cessent.
Entre les arbres, dont les verts sommets le pressent,
Le ciel est blanc ainsi qu'une rue à Tunis.
Le parfum des œillets, du benjoin et des lis
Fait autour des jardins de flottantes tonnelles.
Le jour luit comme un char que traînent cent mille ailes!
La douce, palpitante et plaintive chaleur
A soif comme un sillon, comme un gosier de fleur,
Comme un enfant qui court dans un jardin d'Espagne.
Ô sécheresse ardente enflammant la campagne!
L'air est vide, la vie est retirée au loin
Dans la fraîcheur des bois, de la vigne, du foin,
Près de la source où l'air s'ébat et semble humide...
– Mais moi, ô Sécheresse, ô ma jaune Numide,
Ô tireuse de l'arc, guerrière de l'été,
Je veux toucher ta joue et ton cœur dilaté,
Ta blancheur qui ressemble au beau temple d'Égine,
Qui ressemble au vol blanc des cigognes de Chine,
Aux Bouddhas assoupis dont les mains sont en or,
À l'immense chaleur des places de Louqsor,
Aux mers de Marmara lumineuses et chaudes,
Aux marchés de Turquie où tant de fièvre rôde,
Où le besoin de boire est un si dur désir
Qu'une pastèque fait sangloter de plaisir!
À Téhéran qui gonfle et balance ses dômes,
À Mossoul qui se meurt sous des baisers d'aromes,

POEM ON THE AZURE

Gasping for breath, the summer day stands by
Beneath the arrogant white porcelain sky,
Choked by the heat... A saffron veil consumes
Everything, burning, musing on a flume's
Invisible, torrential acid course...
Breaths, gusts, songs, murmurs—undone now their force—
Grow slow, creep to a halt... And then, between
The trees, pressing their topmost branches green
Against the sky, one sees it through the heat's
Dry air, white as bare, dusty Tunis streets.
Lilies, carnations, benzoin... Scents of flowers
Hover aloft like floating orchard bowers.
Daylight, like chariot drawn by myriad wings,
Shines bright... The heat, with plaintive mutterings,
Throbs its thirst like an arid furrow, or
Like a young lad, fleet-footed, making for
A Spanish garden. Drought cast far and wide,
Searing the dry and torrid countryside!
Empty the air... All life has flown its way,
Fled to the woods, the cool vines, to the hay,
The brooklet spring, where breezes, moist in shade,
Yet play... —But you, O Drought, Numidian maid
Of tawny race, who draw the bow, who fight
The summer's battles... How I wish I might
Caress your cheek and touch your welling heart,
Turned stark white as Aegina's temple-art,
White as a flight of China swans; as those
Gold-handed Buddhas dozing their repose;
As Luxor's vast-spread heat; as glistening seas
Of Marmora; as Turkish merchantry's
Bazaars, where such a fever fires the air,
Such thirst, that seeing a simple melon there
Brings sobs of joy and pleasure; white, as well,
As Tehran, with mosque-domes that seem to swell
And sway in the hot breath; as Mosul, spent

Où l'on voudrait, frappant un azur submergeant,
Lever contre le ciel des boucliers d'argent!
– Mais qu'importe, chaleur, ta force âpre et cruelle?
C'est toi la vie ardente, avide, sensuelle!
C'est toi qui rends soudain sulfureux et strident
Le doux bord alangui des routes d'Occident;
C'est toi qui viens briller sur les stores de toile
Comme une matinale et souveraine étoile,
Toi qui fais éclater comme un fruit de Blidah
Les timides volets des blanches vérandas,
Qui fais qu'un mol étang où quelque barque chôme
Devient plus langoureux que les rives de Côme,
Et que le cœur, enfin, lumineux, écarté,
S'enivre de loisirs, de mort, de volupté,
D'âcres langueurs, de feu, de secrets, de phosphore,
Comme un blanc cimetière ouvert près du Bosphore...

And dying from the kiss of pungent-scent
Perfumes, in deep abyss, where one would wield
Against the azure many a silver shield!
–And yet, why care how brash, how rude to us
You are, O heat! Yours is the sensuous,
Passionate power of living! You, who suddenly
Transform with hot, sulphurous stridency
The calm paths of the West, tranquil, serene;
You, who come flashing on the cool shagreen
Blinds covering our windows, in a blaze
Of sovereign majesty, like dawning day's
Bright star; who crackle the irresolute
Verandah-shutters–shy, white–like a fruit
Ripened beneath the Blidah sky; who cause
A placid pond, where lolling barque will pause
In peace, to churn still more than Como's lake,
Languorously, and who at length will make
The heart, glowing and set apart, become
Drunk on voluptuous bliss, on pleasuredom,
On leisure, secrets, death... Heart luminescent,
Drunk on fire, bitter yearnings phosphorescent,
On life, spread wide beside, behind, before,
Like a white graveyard by the Bosphorus' shore...

Lines 26-107: Most of the places in this sun-drenched mini-travelogue–the Egyptian Luxor, the Turkish Marmora, the Iranian Tehran, the Italian Como–need no identification. Perhaps less common is Aegina, one of the Saronic Islands of Greece (whose "beau temple d'Egine" could refer to any of several temples on the island, among them the famous temple to Aphaia), Blidah, a picturesque Algerian town, and Mosul, on the Tigris in Iraq, close to the site of the biblical Nineveh. (Trans.)

LA BEAUTÉ DU PRINTEMPS

Ainsi, quand j'aurai dit combien je vous adore,
Combien je vous désire et combien je t'attends,
Ivresse de l'année, ineffable Printemps,
Tu seras plus limpide et plus luisant encore
Que mon rêve volant, éclatant et chantant!

Les délicats sureaux et la pervenche blanche
Me surprendront ainsi que des yeux inconnus,
Les lilas me seront plus vivants et plus nus,
Le rosier plus empli du parfum qu'il épanche,
Et le gazon plus droit, plus lisse et plus ténu;

La juvénile odeur, aiguë, acide, frêle,
Des feuillages naissants, tout en vert taffetas,
Sera plus évidente à mon vif odorat
Que n'est aux dents le goût de la fraise nouvelle,
Que n'est le poids charmant des bouquets dans les bras.

Devant un si fécond et si profond spectacle,
Je resterai les doigts disjoints, le cœur épars,
Sentant que le bonheur me vient de toute part,
Que chaque grain de terre a fait le doux miracle
D'être un peu de pistil, de corolle et de nard.

– Ainsi, même en t'aimant autant que je vous aime,
Même en ayant, depuis son enfance, voulu
D'un chant délicieux, secret, puissant, goulu,
Consacrer ta douceur et ta grâce suprême,
On ne peut exprimer combien tu nous as plu!

On ne peut pas avoir d'assez vive mémoire,
Ô mon cher mois de mai, que vous ne nous disiez:
« Je suis encor plus beau! Voyez mes cerisiers,
Voyez mes verts îlots qui flottent sur la Loire,
Entendez les oiseaux de mon brûlant gosier!»

SPRING'S BEAUTY

When I have told you how much I adore
And yearn for you, O long-awaited Spring–
You, the year's drunken rite, tongue-challenging–
Then will you still more limpid be, shine more,
Than my dream, burst aloft, borne on song's wing.

Frail elder bushes, periwinkles white,
Will catch me by surprise like strange eyes gazing;
Lilac will seem more lively–naked quite–
Rosebush, more fragrance-filled, dripping delight;
More smooth the slender grass, its straight blades raising;

The newborn greenery's slight, child-fresh savor–
Acid-tart in its taffeta array–
Will even more on my keen senses weigh
Than on my teeth the young strawberry's flavor,
Or on my arms the charms of bloom-bouquet.

Before a sight so fecund, so profound,
I will lie, fingers spread, heart endlessly
Tuned to the miracle engulfing me,
To see each grain of earth flower the ground
With pistil, spike, corolla panoply.

–And yet, for all I love you, I confess
That, though from childhood we would honor thus
With secret, joyous song–strong, sensuous–
Your sweetness and your grace's peerlessness,
Scarce can we tell how much you pleasured us!

Dear month of May, we hear, however far
We turn the sharp ear of our memories:
"How fair am I! Look! See my cherry trees,
My isles of green that float over the Loire,
And heed my ardent throat's bird-melodies!"

Et je le vois, un clair, un frais, un chaud vertige
Fait plier le branchage et ses bourgeons naïfs;
Une vapeur d'extase émane des massifs;
On sent irradier de la plus humble tige
Quelque parfum hardi, insistant, incisif...

– Puisque mes mots chargés de pollens et d'aromes,
Puisque mes chants, toujours troublés jusques aux pleurs
Ô mon Printemps divin, n'auront pas le bonheur
De pouvoir égaler la saveur de tes baumes,
Je m'arrête et soupire au milieu de tes fleurs.

Je te dédie alors ma cinquième année,
Le temps où mes chapeaux ombrageaient mes genoux,
Où mon front était haut comme les seigles roux,
Où mes jeux s'endormaient sur ton herbe fanée,
Où mon cœur infini battait à petits coups;

Le temps où, pressentant ce que serait ma vie,
J'honorais ma tristesse et ma frêle beauté,
Et, les deux bras croisés sur ma robe d'été,
J'écoutais, effrayée, amoureuse et ravie,
Le bruit que fait l'immense et vague Volupté...

There do I see the dizzying heat bend low
The limbs, bud-laden in simplicity,
Clear, fresh... Each mound wafts clouds of ecstasy;
We sense the humblest stem and twig that blow
A bold perfume all round, sharp-pointedly...

—But since my pollen-words, sweet and intense,
Aroma-rich; my tearful songs—O my
Springtime divine!—never, hard though I try,
Will equal your balm's calm and savory scents,
I stop among your flowers, and heave a sigh...

The tot I was at five? Willed to you now...
When broad brims shaded my knees from the heat,
When reached, low as the ruddy rye, my brow,
When frolics on your seared grass dozed somehow,
And my heart, boundless, throbbed its gentle beat;

The time when, sensing what would be my life,
I prized my beauty, sadly spiritless,
And, with my arms crossed on my summer dress,
I listened, full of love and fear, awe-rife,
To sounds of a vast, vague Voluptuousness...

MATIN LYRIQUE

O fraîche et vive promenade!
L'azur est parfumé de thym;
J'écoute dans l'air, ce matin,
Monter un chant de l'Iliade!
– Déesse qui prends par la main
Les guerriers aux belles chlamydes,
Soutiens aussi mes pas timides
Qui tremblent sur le vert chemin.
Déjà tu t'éveilles, tu bouges;
Ah! donne-moi le plus joyeux
De tes héros impétueux,
Le Péléide aux lèvres rouges!
Fais bondir vers mon clair regard,
Par la route jaune et salée
Qui longe la vague gonflée,
Un jeune conducteur de char,
Luisant de soleil, de buée,
N'ayant que les dieux pour rivaux,
Et pressant de cris ses chevaux
Amassés comme des nuées!...

LYRICAL MORNING

O morning stroll, cool, crisp! And there,
In the thyme-scented azure, I
Listen as, reaching toward the sky,
An *Iliad* canto fills the air.
–Goddess who, hand in hand, will ply
Your way with warriors fine-arrayed,
Hold me up as I tremble by,
Timid, along the green arcade.
See? Now you move... Now you awake...
Ah! Give me the most joyous, most
Intrepid hero of the host:
Red-lipped, Peleus's son! Pray, make
Unto my clear-eyed gaze appear,
Over the gold-brined path, beside
The swelling of the teeming tide,
A young, sun-gleaming charioteer,
Glistening, clad in vapor-shrouds,
Rival to gods, a paragon
Shouting his horses on and on,
Each on the other, like the clouds...

Line 12: The reference is to Achilles, son of Peleus, one of the Argonauts who joined Jason in his quest for the Golden Fleece. (Trans.)

LA NOSTALGIE

Vous êtes maintenant le meilleur de ma vie,
Ô mes jours qui passez;
Vous êtes ma jeunesse et ma chère folie,
Vous êtes si pressés!

Lorsque je vais, jouant entre toutes les choses,
Chaque moment me dit:
« Voici que je te laisse un peu moins de ta rose
Et de ton paradis. »

Ah! que déjà s'effeuille entre mes deux mains ivres
Le rosier rose et blanc!
Que déjà midi soit proche!—Pouvoir revivre
Mes premiers jours si lents!

– Avoir quinze ans, rêver dans l'herbe haute et chaude
Où le soleil s'ébat,
Sans se lever pour voir si le bel Amour rôde,
Si l'on entend ses pas!

Savoir que l'on aura, pour posséder le monde,
Tous les autres étés,
Et goûter cette joie insensible et profonde
D'être sans volupté!

Savoir que c'est demain et non pas ce soir même
Que tout sera si beau;
Ne pouvoir distinguer, tant l'azur est suprême,
Les pierres du tombeau!

Croire qu'on ne peut pas épuiser sa jeunesse,
Rire sur les chemins,
S'arrêter pour peser l'infini et l'ivresse,
Baiser ses propres mains...

NOSTALGIA

O days gone by, you are the best of me,
Days who go flying past;
You are my youth, my sweet, mad deviltry:
Why must you fly so fast?

When I go frolicking I hear time say:
"See how, in but a trice,
I steal a bit more of your rose away,
And of your paradise."

Betwixt my drunken hands the rosebud, white
And pink, fritters and frays!
Already noon! Ah, if only I might
Relive youth's long-drawn days!

—To be fifteen, to lie dreaming in hot,
High grass, with sun a-mumming,
Not even stand to see if—or if not—
Love's footsteps might be coming!

To know that, to possess the world, you own
Summers galore; to guess
The taste of joy when love is little known,
Or passion's lustfulness!

To know that everything will lovely be
Tomorrow, not tonight;
And, in the azure glow, not even see
The grave against the light!

Gaily to think your youth is limitless,,
Through endless journey-lands...
Stop, gauge the infinite, weigh drunkenness,
And, laughing, kiss your hands...

Mais maintenant nos cœurs ne peuvent plus attendre,
Leur force pâlira;
Le moment le plus beau, le plus vif, le plus tendre,
Il est entre nos bras.

Je regarde le soir qui gagne les platanes;
Ô bel été du soir,
Combien de fois avant que le bonheur se fane
Viendrai-je ici m'asseoir?

Je pense à vous, passé, loisirs, douces années,
Main faible qui jouait,
Imagination qui fut tant étonnée,
Et pleine de souhaits.

– Ah! par ces nuits d'été, dans l'Orient immense,
Être un cœur qui s'éveille, une âme qui commence!
Être encore une enfant qui rêve et qui attend
Dans un petit jardin de l'antique Ispahan...

But now our hearts can wait no more, their strength
        Weakens and wanes apace;
Moments most gentle, fair, alive, at length,
        Lie in our arms' embrace.

I watch, O summer eve, as your soft shades
        On plantain tops appear;
How many times, before happiness fades,
        Will I be sitting here?

I think of you, years past, and pastimes' pleasure,
        Hands at play, weak of touch,
Imagination, awed beyond all measure,
        And that desired so much.

–Summer nights! Orient, vast world apart...
        To be a soul at birth, a waking heart,
Yet still a child who waits, dreams on and on,
        In gardened nook of fabled Ispahan!

HERMIONE

Ah! que n'ai-je pu vivre au temps sacré des Dieux,
Dans un jardin limpide et léger de Colone,
Buvant l'azur, foulant de mes pieds radieux
L'ombre d'un noir cyprès sur la blanche anémone!

Que n'ai-je pu dîner aussi chez Agathon,
Ou bien, dansant la nuit près des feux de la rade,
Me mêler, le front ceint de roses en bouton,
Au cortège amoureux qui suivait Alcibiade!

J'aurais vécu, portant une cruche de grès,
Me reposant au bord odorant des fontaines,
Écoutant le vent bleu chanter dans les agrès
Quand le soir ramenait les vaisseaux près d'Athènes.

Miracle des jours grecs, que je vous eusse aimé!
J'aurais vu, quand le saule au vent d'été s'écarte,
Petite fille, avec son cœur encor fermé,
Jouer dans un jardin Hermione de Sparte...

HERMIONE

Oh, to have lived those days of many a god
In some Colonna garden, languidly
Sipping the sky, and treading–splendor-shod–
Cypress's shade on white anemone!

Why dined I not with Agathon, well-fed,
Or danced night's fire-lit portside revelries,
Or joined–my brow with rosebuds garlanded–
Those lovers haunting Alcibiades!

Stone pitcher on my head, I would have come
To rest a bit by fountains ringed around
With scents, and listened to the blue winds' hum
Through riggings of those vessels Athens-bound

How I would love you, Greek days' mystery!
When summer breeze would part the willow, swaying,
–Little girl, heart untried–there would I see
Sparta's Hermione, in flowerbeds playing...

Hermione, princess of Sparta, a more shadowy figure than most of those caught up in the Trojan War, was the daughter of Helen of Troy and King Menelaus. As such she would supposedly be at home among the characters Agathon and Alcibiades, in Plato's Symposium, as the Grecian poet herself claims she too would have been. (Trans.)

LA PREMIÈRE AUBÉPINE

Il faisait frais encor, je ne m'attendais pas,
    Aubépine adorable,
À voir se balancer à l'entour de mes pas
    Ton ombre sur le sable.

Mais j'ai levé la tête, et ta sublime odeur
    Sur mon front s'abandonne.
Juliette n'a pas plus d'amour dans le cœur
    Au verger de Vérone!

Je tremble, je m'arrête et je te tends les bras,
    Vanille sur la branche!
Est-ce donc cette fois que ta langueur fera
    Mourir mon corps qui penche?

Hélas! on n'est jamais averti contre vous,
    On ne peut se défendre;
Quelles armes prend-on contre un parfum si doux
    Dont le cœur va se fendre?

Et vous avez l'air bon, simple, calme, ingénu,
    Attirant les abeilles;
On ne peut soupçonner qu'un calice ténu
    Ait des forces pareilles.

Se peut-il, chère fleur, que vous vous complaisiez
    À ce jeu qui transperce?
Que n'ai-je sur mon cœur un bouclier d'osier,
    Comme un soldat de Perse!

Inépuisable odeur, qui nous lie et nous tient
    Jusqu'à ce qu'on se pâme,
Il n'est pas de plus doux et de pire entretien
    Que d'écouter votre âme.

THE FIRST HAWTHORN

Still cool the season, beauteous hawthorn blooming...
I scarcely thought to greet
You on the sands, or see your shadow looming
Breeze-ruffled, at my feet.

But suddenly I sense my brow beset
With heavenly scents thereof;
Nor, in Verona's orchard, was Juliet
Filled with more heartfelt love!

Trembling, I stop. Vanillin-limbed, that bough
That I stoop to caress...
Strength bedimmed, will my life be ended now
In your languorousness?

Alas, we have no warning, no defense
To guard ourselves from you!
What arms are there against a redolence
That breaks the heart in two?

And you–simple, calm innocence!... You, good
And guiltless host to bees...
Who would suspect a frail corolla could
Ever wreak feats like these!

Can you enjoy your sport, the power you wield
To pierce hearts captivated?
Like Persian soldier, why have I no shield,
Tight-knit, of wicker plaited?

Deathless aroma, seizing, tethering us
Till we swoon! Such your toll:
No converse sweeter–nor more dangerous!–
Than listening to your soul!

Ah! les dieux soient loués! Vous allez défleurir,
Car les jours se dépêchent...
Mais l'Amour a déjà, de vos mortels soupirs,
Enduit ses dures flèches!

Praised be the gods, your flowers will soon be dying
As the season departs.
But Love, already, with your deadly sighing,
Has poison-dipped his darts!

DESTINÉE

Celles qui veulent bien n'avoir pas de bonheur
S'entretiennent avec leur belle conscience,
Et goûtent le plaisir, le calme et la science
Dans le temple léger et doré de leur cœur...

Mais quand on est la vie et la douceur suprême,
Quand c'est notre sagesse et le plus beau destin
D'être pleine d'azur, de rayons et de thym,
D'être joyeuse, heureuse et malheureuse même;

Quand, aux instants secrets des crépuscules blancs,
L'âme, toute mêlée à l'univers immense,
Semble, dans son antique et neuve impatience,
Attendre le bonheur depuis trente mille ans;

Quand, tandis que l'on songe au bord de la fenêtre,
L'Été mol et fleuri, et qui ne cède pas,
Dans l'ombre langoureuse avance pas à pas,
Et partout chaudement et fortement pénètre,

Quand on est un jardin enduit de douce glu,
Quand le cœur, plus courbé qu'une branche penchante
Est une tiède nuit où le rossignol chante,
Quand on étouffe, enfin, et quand on n'en peut plus...

DESTINY

Those women who would set themselves apart
From happiness loll with their minds at leisure,
Tasting the balm of knowledge's calm pleasure
In the frail, gilded temple of their heart.

But when we are life's sweetness infinite;
When it is our sage, fairer fate to be
Full of sun, azure, thyme... When destiny
Fulfills our joy or even frowns on it;

When, in white twilights' pallid mysteries,
The soul, through the vast cosmos permeating,
Seems, with long-felt or late impatience, waiting
For happiness, through myriad centuries;

When—as we by the window-ledge sit dreaming—
Soft, florid Summer, steaming, rolls along
Over the languid shade; when torrid, strong,
Everywhere its relentless course goes streaming;

When we are a sticky-sweet garden spot;
When the heart—bowed more than a branch low hung—
Is a warm night with nightingale outsung;
When we would yet strive but, stifled, can not...

Line 20: Unless the abrupt ending—or non-ending—of this poem is the result of a banal publication error, it would be tempting to see in it an embodiment of its theme of the destiny of eternal waiting, with no hope of closure... (Trans.)

LES VIVANTS ET LES MORTS

(1913)

"JE ME DÉFENDS DE TOI…"

Je me défends de toi chaque fois que je veille,
J'interdis à mon vif regard, à mon oreille,
De visiter avec leur tumulte empressé
Ce cœur désordonné où tes yeux sont fixés.
J'erre hors de moi-même en négligeant la place
Où ton clair souvenir m'exalte et me terrasse.
Je refuse à ma vie un baume essentiel.
Je peux, pendant le jour, ne pas goûter au miel
Que ton rire et ta voix ont laissé dans mon âme,
Où la plaintive faim brusquement me réclame…
– Mais, la nuit, je n'ai pas de force contre toi,
Mon sommeil est ouvert, sans portes et sans toit.
Tu m'envahis ainsi que le vent prend la plaine.
Tu viens par mon regard, ma bouche, mon haleine,
Par tout l'intérieur et par tout le dehors.
Tu entres sans débats dans mon esprit qui dort,
Comme Ulysse, pieds nus, débarquait sur la grève;
Et nous sommes tout seuls, enfermés dans mon rêve.
Nous avançons furtifs, confiants, hasardeux.
Dans un monde infini où l'on ne tient que deux.
Un mur prudent et fort nous sépare des hommes,
Rien d'humain ne pénètre aux doux lieux où nous sommes.
Les bonheurs, les malheurs n'ont plus de sens pour nous;
Je recherche la mort en pressant tes genoux,
Tant mon amour a hâte et soif d'un sort extrême,
Et tu n'existes plus pour mon cœur, tant je t'aime!
Mon vertige est scellé sur nous comme un tombeau.
– Ce terrible moment est si brûlant, si beau,
Que, lorsque lentement l'aube teint ma fenêtre,
C'est en me réveillant que je crois cesser d'être…

"WAKING, I BAN YOU FROM MY KEN..."

Waking, I ban you from my ken. I do
Not let myself give eye or ear to you
Or pay heed, with their tumult of the senses,
To your chaos of heart-glance eloquences.
I wander, out of body, paying no
Mind to that goal where, to my weal and woe,
Your memory, in my soul, raises me up
And casts me down. For me, no honeyed cup,
No lingering balm left by your voice, your laughter:
Only that plaintive hunger, chasing after...
—But come night and I can resist no more.
My sleep lies open to the skies—no door,
No roof—and you lay siege to me, invade
My being, subdue me like the meadow laid
Before the gale... You seep in through my eyes,
My lips, my breath, attack Ulysses-wise,
Barefoot, striding the shore—no blare, no din—
Capturing all that lies without, within
My sleeping soul. And we two—only we,
Trapped in my dream—go edging furtively,
Confidently despite the risk, toward that
Infinity, where lies a habitat
For two alone... A wall, imperious,
Wisely and stoutly built, separates us
From all mankind; no human bane, no boon
Reaches our refuge... Ah! Let death come soon
As, nestling my head in your lap, I wait,
Thirsting for fate extreme and swift. So great
My heart's love that you scarce can find the room
To hold it all; and vanish!... Like a tomb,
My dizziness seals us together; then,
Our final instant's flaming awe... And when
Dawn tints my window, I awake to see
That moment when it seems I cease to be...

LA DOULEUR

Quand la douleur est vaste, ardente, sans mélange,
Quand elle aveugle ainsi qu'un ténébreux soleil,
Elle est dans l'eau qu'on boit et dans le pain qu'on mange,
Et dans les rideaux du sommeil!

Comme l'odeur du sel sur les routes marines,
Comme les chauds parfums de Corse ou d'Orient,
Elle emplit le poumon, étourdit la narine,
Et griffe ainsi qu'un diamant!

Les arceaux de l'azur, le fier tranchant des cimes,
La longueur des cités et leurs hauts monuments,
Ne sont qu'une eau rampante et qu'un grisâtre abîme
Auprès de son envolement!

– Douleur qui me comblez, chantez, voix infinie!
Attachez à mon cou vos froids colliers de fer.
Qu'importent l'esclavage et la dure agonie!
Je vois les mondes entr'ouverts.

J'ai vu l'immensité moins vaste que mon être,
L'espace est un noyau que mon cœur contenait,
Je sais ce qu'est avoir, je sais ce qu'est connaître,
J'englobe ce qui meurt et naît!

L'ange qui fit rêver Jésus sur la montagne,
Qui lui montra le monde et tenta son esprit,
M'a, dans les calmes soirs des verdâtres campagnes,
Tout soupiré et tout appris!

Serai-je désormais l'ermite magnanime
Qui vit de son secret, par-delà les humains?
Pourrai-je conserver, dédaigneuse victime,
La solitude de mes mains?

PAIN

When pain is constant, burning, wide outspread,
When it blinds, sun-like, through the shadows' umber,
We taste it in our water, in our bread,
And in the folds that drape our slumber!

Like seascapes' salt-perfume—the Orient's,
Or Corsica's hot fragrance, pungent, stark—
It fills the lungs and awes the nostrils' sense,
And, like a diamond, claws its mark!

The azure vaults, blade-summits rising steep,
Long cities, towers' lofty eminence:
Mere stagnant water, drab pit plunging deep,
Compared to its bedevilments!

—Pain, you who fill me! Sing, voice infinite!
Lay on me your chill iron yoke, clamped fast.
What matter bondage and the grief of it!
Before my glimpse whole worlds lie cast.

More vast my being than the immensity
Of space: nugget my heart held tight inside...
Possessing, knowing... Both well known to me,
For, in me, death and birth abide.

The angel who made Jesus dream upon
The mount, who tried his soul and showed him life,
Taught everything to me with sighs long-drawn
On evenings calm and verdure-rife!

Will I, henceforth, the generous hermit be
Who lives her secret in unpeopled lands?
Or, scornful victim, will I, selfishly,
Keep for myself my fecund hands?

Pourrai-je, quand résonne, ô Printemps, ta cadence,
Ivre du seul orgueil et des seules pitiés,
Écouter la secrète et chaste confidence
        Qui va des soleils à mes pieds?

Ô Douleur! je comprends, arrêtez vos batailles
Au travers de mes pleurs j'entrevois vos projets;
Un chaud pressentiment m'éblouit et m'assaille;
        C'est dans ce feu que je plongeais!

Je sais,–moi qui vous tiens, vous; respire, vous touche,
Moi qui vis contre vous et qui bois votre vin
Dans un dur gobelet collé contre ma bouche,–
        Quel est votre dessein divin;

Vous préparez la vie avec vos sombres armes,
Le corps que vous brisez rêve d'éternité,
Hélas! les purs sanglots, les tremblements, les larmes
        Aspirent à la volupté!

Will I—drunk only on pride's pitying *gestes*,
O Spring, when life echoes your throbbing beat—
Hearken to secrets chaste that come to rest,
Born of the suns, about my feet?

Enough, O Pain! Lay down your arms! I see,
Dim through my tears, the triumph you have planned;
A fire, foreboding, dazzles, staggers me.
I plumbed it, and I understand!

I know—I who inhale you, feel you; oh
Yes, I who live amidst you, drink your wine
From goblet cruel pressed to my lips—I know
The object of your plan divine;

Your weapons dour prepare us; while our broken
Body dreams life eternal, past all measure,
We, alas, trembling, sobbing pleas unspoken,
Yearn for the bliss of fleshly pleasure!

"Ô MON AMI, SOUFFREZ..."

Ô mon ami, souffrez, je saurai par vos larmes,
Par vos regards éteints, par votre anxiété,
Par mes yeux plus puissants contre vous que des armes,
Par mon souffle, qui fait bouger vos volontés,

Par votre ardente voix qui s'élève et retombe,
Par votre égarement, par votre air démuni,
Que ma vie a sur vous cet empire infini
Qui vous attache à moi comme un mort à sa tombe!

Ô mon ami, souffrons, puisque jamais le cœur
Ne convainc qu'en ouvrant plus large sa blessure;
Puisque l'âme est féroce, et puisqu'on ne s'assure
De l'amour que par la douleur!

"O MY FRIEND, SUFFER..."

O my friend, suffer, for thus will I know–
By your wan glance, your tears, anxious, intense,
By my gaze, which you offer no defense,
By my breath that commands your to-and-fro,

By your voice, burning, that will rise and fall,
By your vague air, your look's defenselessness–
That my life rules and holds you, powerless,
Like a corpse tethered to the tomb, in thrall!

O my friend, let us suffer, for the heart
Convinces not, save when the wound gapes grand;
Since fierce the soul, and since love needs pain's hand
    To feel for sure its sting and smart!

"AVOIR TOUT ACCUEILLI..."

Avoir tout accueilli et cesser de connaître!
J'avais le poids du temps, la chaleur de l'été,
Quoi donc? Je fus la vie, et je vais cesser d'être
Pendant toute l'éternité!

J'ai voulu vivre afin d'épuiser mon courage,
Afin d'avoir pitié, afin d'aimer toujours,
Afin de secourir les humains d'âge en âge,
Puisque l'ambition n'est qu'un plus long amour...

– Un bondissant désir comme un torrent me gagne.
Ah! que je hante encor le sommet des montagnes,
Que je livre mes bras aux vents de l'Occident;
Le vert genévrier de ses senteurs me grise,
Un frein couvert d'écume éclate entre mes dents,
Se pourrait-il vraiment que l'univers détruise
Ce qu'il a fait de plus ardent!

"TO HAVE ACCEPTED..."

To have accepted all life's gifts, then, by
And by, be done! I felt time's weight on me,
And summer's heat. Ah! I was life, yet I
    Must die, for all eternity!

I should have lived to use up all my share
Of pluck, affection, pity, ceasing never
To serve mankind from age to age; for, where
There is ambition, there is love forever...

Bounding, a flood of passion stirs, excites
My soul! Oh, that I might still haunt the heights,
The mountaintops, reach out my arms, caress
The Westwind's breath! The juniper's fresh scent
Dizzies me, panting, frothing, bridleless...
What? Can the universe be so intent
    To waste its ardentmost success!

"TU RESSEMBLES À LA MUSIQUE..."

Tu ressembles à la musique
Par la détresse du regard,
Par l'égarement nostalgique
De ton sourire humble et hagard;

Les plus avides mélodies
Qui me boivent le sang du cœur,
N'ont pas de forces plus hardies
Que ta faiblesse et ta pâleur.

Les lumières dans les églises
Ont le même rayonnement
Que ton visage, où je me grise
Du goût d'un nouveau sacrement.

– Tu n'es qu'un enfant qui défaille,
Mais, par les rêves de mon cœur,
Tu ressembles à la bataille,
À Jésus parmi les docteurs,
Aux héros morts sous les murailles,
À tout ce qui lutte et tressaille
Au Cid sur un cheval dansant,
Au martyr, dans le Colisée,
Sur qui la bête, harassée,
Passe, comme un linge apaisant
Tout trempé d'amour et de sang,
Sa langue calme et reposée...

"YOU ARE LIKE MUSIC..."

You are like music to my eyes,
With glance and gaze nostalgia-wrought,
With those faraway looks that rise
Out of your smile, humble, distraught;

Melodies most intense, that drain
My very blood, are not so hale
Or whole–bold though their efforts vain–
As is your weakness, wan and pale.

Churches' lights spread their gentle gleam
With quite the same resplendent shine
As does your face, where, drunk, I seem
To taste new sacrament divine.

Only a faltering child are you,
But in my heart's dream you appear
A fighter, like a Jesus, who
Roused the Church Doctor retinue;
Dead heroes at the walls; all those
Who struggle, trembling, in the throes
Of lancing blow and doughty deed;
El Cid, upon his dancing steed;
The Coliseum martyr, bled,
Whose wounds his victim-beast would dress–
Covered with love though bloodied red–
With its tongue's healing, calm caress...

Line 20: El Cid is the national hero of medieval Christian Spain in its victory over the Moorish invaders. Don Rodrigo Díaz de Vivar (1043-1099), known as "El Cid Campeador" ["the champion"], is the protagonist of the anonymous epic *El Cantar de Mío Cid.* (Trans.)

Lines 20-24: The reference is clearly to the famous tale of Androcles and the Lion, originally recounted as true by Aulus Gellius, also found in Aesop, and eventually the inspiration for Shaw's comedy of the same name. (Trans.)

"SI VOUS PARLIEZ, SEIGNEUR..."

Si vous parliez, Seigneur, je vous entendrais bien,
Car toute humaine voix pour mon âme s'est tue,
Je reste seule auprès de ma force abattue,
J'ai quitté tout appui, j'ai rompu tout lien.

Mon cœur méditatif et qui boit la lumière
Vous aurait absorbé, si, transgressant les lois,
Comme le vent des nuits qui pénètre les pierres
Votre verbe enflammé fût descendu sur moi!

Nul ne vous souhaitait avec tant d'indigence;
Je vous aurais fêté au son du tympanon
Si j'avais, dans mon triste et studieux silence,
Entendu votre voix et connu votre nom.

Si forte qu'eût été l'ombre sur vos visages,
Sublime Trinité! j'eusse écarté la nuit,
Mon esprit vous aurait poursuivie sans ennui,
Et j'aurais abordé à votre clair rivage.

Mais jamais rien à moi ne vous a révélé,
Seigneur! ni le ciel lourd comme une eau suspendue,
Ni l'exaltation de l'été sur les blés,
Ni le temple ionien sur la montagne ardue;

Ni les cloches qui sont un encens cadencé,
Ni le courage humain, toujours sans récompense,
Ni les morts, dont l'hostile et pénétrant silence
Semble un renoncement invincible et lassé;

Ni ces nuits où l'esprit retient comme une preuve
Son aspiration au bien universel;
Ni la lune qui rêve, et voit passer le fleuve
Des baisers fugitifs sous les cieux éternels.

"IF YOU SPOKE, LORD..."

If you spoke, Lord, I would give ear to you,
For now no human voice speaks to my soul;
Alone, I lie beside my strength, unwhole,
Unbound, with nothing left to huddle to.

My pondering heart–thirsting for light, and bred
On pensive mood–if life's laws held not fast,
Would have drunk deep, like rocks in night-wind's blast,
Had your flame-words descended on my head!

None sought you in such misery! How might
I fete you, drum the tympanum, rejoice,
If, in my silence sad, glum, erudite,
I could but know your name, hear your own voice!

Though shadow-veiled your faces, Trinity
Sublime, I would have swept the darkness, for
My spirit would have sought you willingly,
That I might anchor at your shining shore.

But never you revealed yourself to me!
Not in the summer's lust in fields of corn,
Nor in the sky, hung like a weighty sea,
Nor in Ionian temple, summit-borne;

Not in the bells, their incense-rhythm peeling;
Nor in man's courage that no prize can boast;
Nor in the dead's dour silence cruel, unfeeling,
Who, spent, seem to have given up the ghost;

Not in those nights where spirit proves it can
Ignore the universal good; nor dreaming
Moon in the timeless sky, as river, streaming,
Casts furtive kisses that the heavens span.

Hélas! ni ces matins de ma brûlante enfance,
Où, dans les prés gonflés d'un nuage d'odeur,
Je sentais, tant l'extase en moi jetait sa lance,
Un ange dans les cieux qui m'arrachait le cœur!

Pourtant, ayez pitié! Que votre main penchante
Vienne guider mon sort douloureux et terni;
J'aspire à vous, Splendeur, Raison éblouissante!
Mais je ne vous vois pas, ô mon Dieu! et je chante
A cause du vide infini!

Alas! Not in those childhood dawns that smart
And burn in swelling scent-cloud fields, where I
Would feel—as ecstasy its lance let fly—
A heavenly angel ripping at my heart!

But pity, pray! May your hand, succoring,
Come guide my fate from the pain wilting it,
I yearn for you, O Reason splendoring,
But see you not, dear God mine! And I sing
    The emptiness, vast, infinite...

“MON DIEU, JE SAIS QU’IL FAUT...”

Mon Dieu, je sais qu’il faut accepter la détresse,
Qu’il faut, dans la douleur, descendre jusqu’en bas,
Mais, dans ce labyrinthe où votre main nous presse,
Puisque vous êtes bon, ne se pourrait-il pas
Que nous entrevoyions du moins la claire issue
Que déjà votre main prépare doucement,
Et qu’un peu de lumière, au lointain aperçue,
Nous aide à supporter ce ténébreux moment?

Pourquoi nos maux sont-ils si compacts et si denses
Qu’on semble enseveli dans un obscur caveau?
D’où vient cette funèbre et perfide abondance
Qui submerge le cœur et trouble le cerveau?

Pourtant, les lendemains sont quelquefois si tendres,
On revoit les regards que l’on n’espérait plus.
Mais le bonheur fait mal quand il faut trop l’attendre,
Être sauvés enfin, ce n’est plus être élus.

Consolez-nous parfois dans cette forteresse
Dont vous tenez les clefs et fermez le vitrail;
Laissez-nous pressentir les futures caresses
Et leur fraîche beauté d’eau bleue et de corail!

C’est trop d’être privé de la douce espérance,
D’être comme un forçat serré le long du mur,
Qui ne peut pas prévoir sa juste délivrance,
Car la fenêtre est haute et les verrous sont durs.

Pourquoi ce faste affreux de l’angoisse où nous sommes
Pourquoi ce deuil royal et ces chagrins pompeux,
Puisqu’il vous plaît parfois d’avoir pitié des hommes
Et de remettre encor le bonheur auprès d’eux?

“DEAR GOD, I KNOW...”

Dear God, I know that we must, valorous,
Accept distress, and to great depths sink low;
But in this maze where your hand presses us,
Can you not, in your goodness and our woe,
Let us at least glimpse from afar the light
That your hands, even now, gently prepare,
So that, however dim, the distant sight
Might lead us through the gloom we now must bear?

Why must our ills be so compact, so dense,
That we seem sunk in caverns’ dark domain?
Whence comes that deadly dole of pestilence
That can submerge the heart, muddle the brain?

Yet our tomorrows may at times be tender;
We see the glances we deemed lost from view.
But happiness delayed is our offender:
Those saved at length are not the chosen few.

Console us in this stained-glass fortress, whose
Keys you hold... Shut the window tight, and let
Our flesh foretaste the water’s corals, blues,
In fresh, cool, sweet-caressing tête-à-tête.

Too cruel it is to be deprived of hope,
To be like prisoner pent, not sure at all
Of being justly saved, a-crawl, a-grope;
Solid the bolts and high the windowed wall.

And why this fearsome pomp about us? Why
This royal mourning, men’s sumptuous duress,
Since you deign pity mankind, by the by,
And, now and then, restore its happiness?

Faut-il donc au Destin ces heures pantelantes,
L'émeut-on par un corps qui tremble et qui gémit?
Nos pleurs sont-ils un peu de cette huile brûlante
Que Psyché répandit sur l'Amour endormi?

S'il se peut, écartez ces moments de la vie
Où nous sommes broyés sous un joug trop étroit,
Et, pareils aux mineurs dans la noire asphyxie,
Nous tentons d'écarter le roc avec nos doigts.

– Déjà, loin du plaisir, du monde, des parades,
Mon cœur ardent n'est plus, dans son éclat voilé,
Qu'un feu de bohémiens sur la pauvre esplanade,
Où l'enfant nu console un cheval dételé.

– Mais s'il faut que ces jours de supplice reviennent,
S'il faut vivre sans eau, sans soleil et sans air,
Que du moins votre main s'empare de la mienne
Et m'aide à traverser l'effroyable désert...

Does Fate demand those panting hours? Is she
Moved by a body trembling, sighing deep?
Do our tears burn, like that oil, silently,
That Psyche dripped on Love, lying asleep?

If you can, sweep aside those times, push back
Those moments when, too tightly yoked, we stand
Like miners, trying in the choking black,
To sweep aside the rock with but one hand.

–Far from life's pleasures and parades, my hot,
Passionate heart, flame-veiled, is nothing more
Than a poor Gypsy campfire, where a tot,
Bare, calms a sad horse, reinless, on the shore.

–But if those torture-days must come again,
If I must live without sun, water, air,
At least pray take my hand in yours, and then
Help me to cross the desert of despair...

Line 32: The mythological reference is to the love affair between Psyche, originally a mortal, and Cupid, who had forbidden her to look upon him during their nocturnal amours. One night, however, too curious, she accidentally let fall a drop of hot oil from her lamp onto his shoulder. Cupid awoke and fled, though eventually he did make Psyche not only his wife but a goddess as well. (Trans.)

"J'AI REVU LA NATURE..."

J'ai revu la Nature en son commencement.
J'entends comme en naissant, comme en ouvrant l'oreille
Un bruit de branches, d'eau, de brises et d'abeilles
Passer avec un vague et frais étonnement.
On voit partout jaillir de la terre âpre et dure
La vapeur balancée et molle des verdures....
– Nature, je connais votre piège éternel:
Forte par la beauté, humble par le silence,
Vous attendez qu'en nous sans cesse recommence
L'immense adhésion au but universel.
L'indiscernable Amour tente un furtif appel...
Je suis là; l'églantier enlace un banc de marbre
Qu'entoure la senteur fourmillante des buis.
Tout gonfle et se fendille avec un léger bruit
De résine au soleil; le vent, au haut des arbres,
A les grands mouvements de l'inspiration.
Hélas! cette salubre et chaste passion,
Ce grand nid des vivants qui croît et se prépare,
Sera-t-il donc toujours l'ennemi des humains?
Parmi ce tourbillon de graines et d'essaims,
Nature, vous faut-il une âme qui s'égare,
Et qui mêle à votre âcre et printanier levain
L'inutile désir d'un amour plus divin,
Que vous désabusez et que rien ne répare?...

"I'VE SEEN NATURE'S BEGINNING..."

I've seen Nature's beginning, at her birth.
Ears open wide, I hear the buzz of bees,
Branches, rustling of water, whistling breeze
Spreading a vague awe, fresh, over the earth.
One sees a soft green mist spurt in the air,
Out of the acrid soil, and hover there...
–Nature, I know your trap eternal, sprung
Upon us! Strong in beauty, humbly mute,
Proffering new beginnings, you recruit
Us for the universal soul, among
Your adepts. Love–unseen, silent of tongue–
Tempts me in furtive guise. There am I found...
A bench of marble stands, with dog-rose laced,
Teeming with boxwood scents, fragrance-embraced.
Everything swells, throbs, crackles with the sound
Of pine-sap in the sun; the winds sweep round
The treetops with gestures inspired. Alas!
Must that chaste passion pure that would amass
A host of humankind, a nest of those
Who live and breathe, a nest to grow and thrive,
Ever be one of mankind's archest foes?
Nature, must you have, if you would survive,
Some lost soul in those whirling storms, those flights
Of grains, swarms, grasses, who, to stay alive,
Mixes amid your bitter leavening–
Bitter, yet not without a hint of spring–
The futile wish for love's celestial heights
That you gainsay and that naught puts to rights?...

"LES VIVANTS SE SONT TUS..."

Les vivants se sont tus, mais les morts m'ont parlé,
Leur silence infini m'enseigne le durable.
Loin du cœur des humains, vaniteux et troublé,
J'ai bâti ma maison pensive sur leur sable.

– Votre sommeil, ô morts déçus et sérieux,
Me jette, les yeux clos, un long regard farouche;
Le vent de la parole emplit encor ma bouche,
L'univers fugitif s'insère dans mes yeux.

Morts austères, légers, vous ne sauriez prétendre
À toujours occuper, par vos muets soupirs,
La race des vivants, qui cherche à se défendre
Contre le temps, qu'on voit déjà se rétrécir;

Mais mon cœur, chaque soir, vient contempler vos cendres,
Je ressemble au passé et vous à l'avenir.
On ne possède bien que ce qu'on peut attendre:
Je suis morte déjà, puisque je dois mourir...

"MUTE ARE THE LIVING..."

Mute are the living, but the dead have spoken.
Their ageless silence teaches me what stands
Unchanged. Far from the human heart–vain, broken–
I've built my pensive dwelling on their sands.

–Your sleep, O Dead, eyes closed in grim, grave wise,
Casts upon me a long and savage glance;
Words' breath yet fills my mouth; the vast expanse
Of fleeting universe invades my eyes.

Dour, fickle Dead! You cannot hope to bend
Time's will, with voiceless sighs, to occupy
Those living yet, who, watching time, defend
Against it, ever shrinking, passing by.

Still, nightly comes my heart here to attend
Your ashes: you, like time to come, and I,
Time past. Ours? What we wait for till the end:
I am already dead, since I must die...

"LA NUIT RAPPROCHE MIEUX..."

Et nous nous regardons tous les deux fixement,
Elle qui brille et moi qui souffre.
–V. Hugo

La nuit rapproche mieux les vivants et les morts;
Dans l'ombre unie et calme où la fraîcheur s'élance
Voici l'heure du rêve épars et du silence.
À l'horizon s'installe, exacte et sans effort,
La lune demi-ronde, amenant autour d'elle
Son cortège glacé, scintillant et fidèle,
Semblable aux feux légers dispersés dans les ports.
– Comme une blanche algèbre énigmatique et triste,
Cette géométrie insondable persiste,
Et fait des cieux du soir un problème éternel...
Mais rien ne vient répondre à nos pressants appels;
Tout trompe nos regards assurés et débiles
Les cieux précipités qui semblent immobiles,
L'ombre qui, sur nos fronts, met sa protection,
Le silence propice aux nobles passions.
– O lune aux flancs brisés, mélancolique amphore
D'où ne coule aucun vin pour les cœurs altérés,
Sur Tarente, Amalfi, sur les rochers sacrés,
Baignant l'œillet marin, les vertes ellébores,
Vous sembliez parfois, d'un regard éthéré,
Secourir notre amère et plaintive indigence,
Mais ce soir je ne sens que votre froid dédain.
– Excitant du désir et de l'intelligence,
Ô lune, accueillez-vous, dans vos pâles jardins,
L'immense poésie ailée et taciturne
Qui mène les esprits par delà les instincts,

"NIGHT BEST BRINGS THOSE..."

And we look at each other, fixed our gaze,
She shining bright, and I in pain.
–V. Hugo

Night best brings those living and dead together;
Now is the silent hour of dreams outspread,
Scattered midst cool, calm shadows... Overhead,
The half-round moon settles, soft as a feather,
On the horizon, poised, precise, whilst in
Her company sparkles–cold, crystalline–
Her faithful retinue. One could ask whether
Their twinklings are lights hung from ships in port:
An algebra of pale and puzzling sort–
Unsolvable, this sad geometry–
Persisting, making of the evening skies
An endless problem for eternity...
But nothing answers our questions, our cries,
Naught that our gaze perceives is as it seems,
Too weak our eyes despite our confidence:
The heavens rush circling round, though our mind deems
Them still; the darkness is our brows' defense,
The silence, our noble desires' ally.
–O split-flanked moon, amphora sadness-cast,
Whence pours no wine for thirsting hearts... Time past,
Set in Taranto's and Amalfi's sky,
Over their sacred cliffs, you seemed to swathe
The sea-carnation, the green hellebore,
In an ethereal glance, whose boon would bathe
To health our woe and bitterness, heart-sore...
No more! Tonight I feel only your chill

Et que nous confions aux espaces nocturnes,
À l'heure où, quand tout bruit et tout éclat s'éteint,
Notre cœur vous choisit comme un appui lointain?...

Mais en vain mon esprit qui souffre et qui réclame
Interroge. – La brise, alerte et tiède, trame
Un tissu délié où les parfums se pâment.
Et je respire avec un cœur exténué
La douce odeur des nuits, qui vient atténuer
Le vide sans espoir où ne sont pas les âmes...

Disdain... O moon, who spawn lust's fire, who will
Ever excite the mind, tell me, in your
Bleak gardens–when all life's concern has run
Its course and all the noise at last is done–
Do you welcome that mute, winged poetry
That guides the soul past instinct, and that one
Entrusts to night's immensity, as we
Lean our heart on your distant sympathy?...

My spirit, in its pain, seeks right and left
For answers... But in vain: the breeze–warm, deft–
Spins out a fabric, swoon-perfumed, loose-weft,
And I inhale, with heart drawn weak and wan,
The sweet night-scents that ply their comforts on
The hopeless emptiness, void, soul-bereft...

Epigraph: The lines that Noailles quotes are from Victor Hugo's poem "Paroles sur la dune" from the collection *Les Contemplations,* a poem whose inspiration is quite close to her own. (Trans.)

"JE NE VEUX PAS SAVOIR S'IL FAIT CLAIR..."

Je ne veux pas savoir s'il fait clair, s'il fait triste,
Si le printemps, exact, va reverdir encor,
Si l'orgueilleux soleil jette son cerceau d'or
Sur les chemins légers de la bleuâtre piste,
Ni si le vif matin a son joyeux ressort,
Et le soir ses couleurs de lin et d'améthyste,
Je sais que pour les morts plus aucun temps n'existe:
    Je suis jalouse pour les morts.

"I DO NOT CARE IF DAYS..."

I do not care if days are sad or bright;
If spring, on schedule, spreads its greening; or
If the sun, haughty, rings–behind, before–
The bluish pathways in its golden light;
Nor if crisp morning crackles gaily; nor
If evening glows, purple and linen-white...
The dead care little for the day, the night:
　　　I envy those who are no more.

LES FORCES ÉTERNELLES

(1920)

LES BORDS DE LA MARNE

La Marne, lente et molle, en glissant accompagne
Un paysage ouvert, éventé, spacieux.
On voit dans l'herbe éclore, ainsi qu'un astre aux cieux,
Les villages légers et dormants de Champagne.

La Nature a repris son rêve négligent.
Attaché à la herse un blanc cheval travaille.
Les vignobles jaspés ont des teintes d'écaille
À travers quoi l'on voit rôder de vieilles gens.

Un automnal buisson porte encor quelques roses.
Une chèvre s'enlace au roncier qu'elle mord.
Les raisins sont cueillis, le coteau se repose,
Rien ne témoigne plus d'un surhumain effort
Qu'un tertre soulevé par la forme d'un corps.

– Dans ce sol, sans éclat et sans écho, s'incarnent
Les héros qui, rompus de fatigue et de faim,
Connaissant que jamais ils ne sauront la fin
De l'épique bataille à laquelle ils s'acharnent,
Ont livré hardiment les combats de la Marne.

La terre les recouvre. On ne sait pas leur nom.
Ils ont l'herbe et le vent avec lesquels ils causent.
Nous songeons.
Par delà les vallons et les monts
On entend le bruit sourd et pâmé du canon
S'écrouler dans l'éther entre deux longues pauses.
Et puis le soir descend. Le fleuve au grand renom,
À jamais ignorant de son apothéose,
S'emplit de la langueur du crépuscule, et dort.

Je regarde, les yeux hébétés par le sort,
La gloire indélébile et calme qu'ont les choses
Alors que les hommes sont morts...

Octobre 1916

THE BANKS OF THE MARNE

Slow-gliding, soft, the Marne meanders far
And wide through Champagne's airy plain, whose earth,
In grassy meadowlands, gives tender birth
To many a sleeping town, like sky-born star.

Nature takes up her idling dream once more.
A white dray horse toils at what horses do.
As vineyards sport a mottled fish-scale hue,
Old folks saunter about from chore to chore.

On autumn bush cling a few roses still.
A goat nibbles the thorns that hem her in.
The grapes are picked, peace slumbers on the hill...
Nothing here marks the carnage that has been,
Save a mound's bulge raised by the corpse within...

–Part of this mute soil now, heroically
In the Marne's epic struggle, famished, spent,
They fought the battle, bold, magnificent,
And know that never will they live to see
The final bitter fruits of victory.

Earth covers them. Their names are nowhere found.
Only the grass and wind know what each says.
We muse...
                    Beyond the hills and valleys round,
One hears the muffled swoon of cannon-sound
Crumbling in air midst long-drawn silences.
Then night descends. The river, vast-renowned
But unaware of triumph's laurelings,
Swells with dusk's languor, tired, and goes to bed.

With a stare stunned by fate, daze-spirited,
I gaze upon the glorious peace that things,
            Changeless, possess when men lie dead...

October 1916

"LE PAYSAGE EST CALME..."

Le paysage est calme et dur,
D'une candeur qui désaltère;
On croit que ce morceau d'azur
Repose sous un globe en verre.

Un cytise se laisse choir
Sur la blanche épine fleurie.
– Écoute les parfums du soir,
Confidences de la prairie!

L'atmosphère est un bleu désert,
Sans rien qui soupire ou qui tremble;
L'herbage mielleux des prés semble
Doucement mâchonné par l'air,

Tant son suc imprègne et sature
D'une exacte et nette liqueur
L'espace peinturé d'odeurs
Et capitonné de verdure!

Sur le divan pâmé du temps,
Le croissant de la lune froide
Jette sa lame, courbe et roide
Comme la dague d'un sultan.

– Je n'ignore rien, ô Nature,
De votre vague immensité,
Je subis la tendre torture
Qu'impose un vaporeux été,

Je sais qu'un invincible abîme
Enlace mes pieds et mon corps,
Et que j'avance vers le crime
Inconcevable de la mort.

"TRANQUIL, THE LANDSCAPE..."

Tranquil, the landscape lies out, hard,
In sly, thirst-quenching white, as in
The air an azure chunk, bell-jarred,
Seems set in a globe crystalline.

Tenderly a laburnum falls
Amid the pale thorns' budding scents:
–Listen as each of them recalls
Many a meadow confidence.

The atmosphere is barren blue
With not a quiver, not a sigh;
The field grass, honey-soft of hue,
Seems gently chewed up by the sky;

So boldly do its juices, steeping
Perfume-limned space, quilted in green–
Liquor precise–imbibe it, seeping
Throughout the air, betwixt, between!

In crescent-curve the dagger moon–
Thrust on the night sky–stiff and cold,
On the divan of Time a-swoon,
Shines like some sultan's blade of old.

–O Nature, far and wide I see
Your broad expanse, and I surrender
To vaporous summer-tortures tender,
And all your vague immensity.

Knowing that the abyss of time,
Invincible, my feet enmeshes,
Drawing me downward to the flesh's
Final enigma, death's dark crime.

– Ô belles choses naturelles!
Que par vous mon rêve a saigné!
Mais par mes chants, tout imprégnés
D'un élixir dont je chancelle,
J'enclave l'homme, dédaigné,
Au sein de la vie éternelle!

Que suis-je? Un humble atome errant,
Dont l'ardeur fut grave et pieuse,
Qui vit le réel d'un œil franc
Voilé de stupeur amoureuse,
Et j'ai rendu, en l'adorant,
L'évidence mystérieuse...

–O wealth of nature's loveliness!
You it is who have bled my dreams!
And yet, the balm my songs express–
Falteringly, I fear–redeems
A mankind scorned, to the caress
Of life eternal, limitless!

What am I but a wandering
And lowly speck, whose piety
Caused me to look on everything–
Veiled by love's stupor–artlessly,
As I would render, worshiping,
The evidence's mystery...

MATIN D'ÉTÉ

Le chaud velours de l'air offre à la rêverie
Un divan duveteux où mon esprit s'ébat,
La verte crudité de la jeune prairie
Est pour l'œil ébloui un exaltant repas.

L'ombrage et le soleil quadrillent la pelouse
Où le brûlant matin se repose, encagé;
Il semble qu'en volant une guêpe recouse
Le merveilleux éther par ses jeux dérangé.
Mon immobile rêve a l'ampleur d'un voyage;
J'entends le bruit mouvant et lointain de l'été,
Murmure énigmatique où tout est volupté.
Le ciel, aride et pur, est comme un bleu dallage,
Mon cœur calme bénit les dieux aériens,
Et je croise les mains, n'ayant besoin de rien
Que de penser à toi dans un clair paysage...

SUMMER MORNING

The air's warm velvet lays out, for my dreaming,
A downy couch for revels of the mind;
The meadow's fresh and untamed green shines, gleaming,
A heady banquet for the eye, sun-blind.

Shadow and light, aligned, map out the lawn
Where lies the sweltering morning, caged; a flitting
Wasp seems to keep restitching–hither, yon–
The glowing ether that its play keeps splitting.
My dream is a vast voyage, motionless;
The summer's distant rustlings strike my ear:
Blissful, the puzzling rumblings that I hear;
Barren, the sky, like azure tiles; I bless
The gods of air with peaceful heart; and I,
Folding my hands, need nothing more than my
Thoughts of you in a landscape's limpidness...

"POUR OUBLIER LA MORNE HOULE..."

Pour oublier la morne houle
Humaine, affairée et frivole,
Écoutons respirer la foule
Des belles choses sans paroles.

Calme du soir, fraîche candeur!
– Que j'aime ces abords des bois
Où gît, invisible et sans poids,
La masse immense des odeurs...

"TO HELP FORGET THE DREARY TIDE..."

To help forget the dreary tide
Of trifling human putterings,
Let's listen to the soft breath, sighed
By hosts of lovely wordless things.

Cool, evening's calm spreads artlessly!
–Oh, how I love these woods, where lies,
Weightless, transparent to the eyes,
The fragrances' immensity...

DANS L'ADOLESCENCE

Je me souviens d'un jour de ma seizième année,
Où, malade et pensant mourir,
Je sentais s'installer sur mon âme étonnée
Le destin qui fait obéir.

Du fond de ma douleur physique et terrassante,
Qu'un médicament apaisait,
J'entendais soupirer ma mère pâlissante,
Qui pleurait et qui se taisait.

Je regardais les cieux par la fenêtre ouverte;
Le cèdre bleu, d'un si haut jet,
Reposait sur le soir ses branchages inertes
Qui semblaient prier. Je songeais.

Des oiseaux aux longs cris allaient rafler dans l'ombre
Les derniers parfums engourdis,
Deux étoiles naissaient, humectant l'azur sombre,
Je me disais: « Le Paradis

C'est de suivre l'oiseau et de joindre l'étoile
Et d'appartenir à l'éther. »
Et mes forces cédaient comme on défait un voile,
Je me mélangeais avec l'air.

J'entendis un râteau faire au bord des pelouses,
Parmi les graviers murmurants,
Son bruit lisse et perlé. Je n'étais pas jalouse
De la vie, en mon cœur mourant!

J'étais astre, feuillage, aile, parfum, nuage,
Doux chant du monde ralenti,
Mon âme recouvrait son tendre parentage
En touchant les cieux arrondis.

IN ADOLESCENCE

I recall, in my sixteenth year, one day
    When, ill and sure I was to die,
Destiny—ever one to have his way—
    Weighed on my soul, I knew not why.

From deep within my body's wrack and woe,
    Medicine-comforted, my ears
Could hear my mother, pallid, sob, then grow
    Silent between her sighs and tears.

The open window let me turn my gaze
    Up to the sky; the cedar fused
Its blue jet, high, on sunset's final rays;
    Its limbs, stilled, seemed to pray. I mused...

Birds with long cry ransacked the shadows, darkling,
    For last lush fragrance, boldly sought;
Two stars, newborn, bedewed the azure, sparkling.
    "It must be Paradise," I thought,

"To join the realm ethereal; to go
    Off with the birds and stars." Then, there,
Like a veil loosed, undone, I stood. And, lo!
    Strength gone, I flew, one with the air.

I heard a rake by lawn's edge, gratingly
    Spread smooth the gravel, chattering;
But my heart, dying, felt no jealousy
    Toward life and its continuing!

I was star, greensward, cloud, wings, perfumed scents—
    Sung slow, the world's sweet, gentle sound;
I found my roots there, in the firmament's
    Embrace, the heavens circling round...

– Puissé-je ainsi mourir, sans crainte et sans supplice,
Le soir calme d'un jour d'été,
Et retrouver, au bruit d'un jardin qu'on ratisse,
Cette païenne sainteté!...

–Oh, that I might die thus–no fear, no pain–
    Some summer eve, calm, effortless,
And find, mid sounds of garden raked again,
    Once more that pagan saintliness...

"JE CROYAIS ÊTRE..."

Je croyais être calme et triste,
Simplement, sans demander mieux
Que ce noble état sérieux
D'un cœur lassé. Le soir insiste:
Avec les glissements du vent,
Et la froide odeur des herbages,
Et cette paix des paysages
Sur qui le désir est rêvant,
Il défait mon repos sans joie,
Ce repos qui protégeait bien,
Il exige, hélas! que je voie
Ces rusés jeux aériens
Où tout s'enveloppe et se pille,
Du sol tiède aux clartés des cieux...
– Pourquoi, soir mol et spongieux
D'où coule un parfum de vanille,
Blessez-vous, dans mon cœur serré
Qui soudain s'entr'ouvre et vacille,
Cette éternelle jeune fille
Qui ne peut cesser d'espérer?

"I THOUGHT THAT TO BE SAD..."

I thought that to be sad was but
My lot; that calm nobility
Of wearied heart was meant to be
My destiny, no matter what.
But night insists: his whistling wind
And the cool scent of grasses, and
This peace that overspreads the land
Fraught with desire and dream... Rescind
His order? He will not! He sweeps
Apart my joyless sleep, persists,
Rouses me from that rest that keeps
Me safe. Imperious egotist's
Demands! Ah, woe is me! He makes
Me watch the clever tricks the air
Will play—high, low, and everywhere—
Engulfing all, where all partakes
In secrecy and plucks its fill.
—O evening of the sponge-soft fingers
Steeped in vanilla scent, why will
You wound that young lass who still lingers,
Tightly clenched in my heart, until
Suddenly she emerges; she
Who must yet hope eternally?

CONSOLATION

Réjouis-toi d'avoir tant souffert, car enfin
Toute fureur ayant son déclin, la détresse
Connaît aussi la lente et paisible paresse
Qui trouve son repos, et n'a ni soif ni faim.

Il n'est pas que la joie et l'espoir qui faiblissent,
La fringante douleur pâlit aussi. Comment
Ne pas goûter du moins, après tant de supplices,
L'absence de l'atroce et neuf étonnement?

Car le pauvre être humain, instruit par la souffrance,
À l'espoir comme au deuil oppose un calme esprit,
L'infortune et la mort n'ont plus rien qui l'offense,
Et c'est vaincre le sort que n'être pas surpris.

CONSOLATION

Be glad that you have suffered greatly, for
No turmoil is there but subsides; distress
Slowly sinks into gentle listlessness
That finds repose, and hungers, thirsts, no more.

Not only joy and hope grow weak; one's pain,
Stinging, will pale no less. For how can one,
After great torment, not know peace again?
Once the first shock is past the worst is done.

Poor humankind, schooled in the ways of woe,
Can bear both hope and grief with calm complete;
Death, dole have no more anguish to bestow;
Not to be shocked: such is fate's best defeat.

MÉDITATION

L'orage est en suspens, l'espace se recueille;
Dans le jardin où brille une vapeur de four,
Les oiseaux ont un cri fané comme une feuille.
Partout gît mollement, fardeau subtil et lourd,
La chaleur insensée qui fait aimer l'amour.
J'ai recherché Ronsard dans la bibliothèque;
Ma chambre, où les volets emprisonnent le jour
Et d'un tranchant léger et laiteux le dissèquent,
A l'obscure fraîcheur d'un tranquille vallon.
Un blanc magnolia, froid comme une pastèque,
Épanche son parfum de neige et de melon,
Et je vois tout cela avec des yeux si tendres
Qu'ils émettent un chant que l'on devrait entendre.
La pendule, incessante autant que l'univers,
Accompagne humblement, seconde par seconde,
Le tumulte secret et céleste des mondes.
Et j'écoute l'énigme obsédante de l'air
Et ce cri des oiseaux emplis d'inquiétude...
– Se pourrait-il, ô cieux, que j'eusse l'habitude
De vivre, de goûter le suave désert
Que forme le repos songeur après l'étude!
Ne sais-je pas qu'assis, ou debout et courant,
L'homme est toujours un même et régulier mourant!
Le Sort, qui le poursuit, ne le guette pas même,
Tant le pauvre vivant est désigné: s'il aime,
Quelque chose toujours lentement se défait
Dans son bonheur craintif, sa détresse ou sa paix;
Il ne peut persister en son choix noble et tendre,
Il lui faut regretter comme il lui faut attendre,
Il ne connaît jamais les vœux du lendemain.
– Et pourtant, moi, le plus combattu des humains,
L'âme la plus souvent par l'orage étonnée,
Qui toujours vis les pleurs au plaisir se mêlant,

MEDITATION

The storm hangs, interrupted, in the air;
Space stops to ponder... In the garden, where
Oven-hot vapor glistens, birdcalls, all
Withered and faded, like leaves wilting, dead...
Everything softly lies: heat's heavy pall–
Senseless with weight, but subtle-spirited–
That makes us fall in love with love... I went
To fetch a volume of Ronsard. My room,
Where daylight, from its shutter-prison pent–
A slight, milk-white-edged blade slicing the gloom–
Stands like a valley, peaceful, cool... Outside,
A white magnolia, melon-fresh, casts wide
Its scents of snow and fruit. With innocent
And tender glance that sings in accents meant
Certainly to be heard, I gaze... The clock's
Unerring beat–firm as the universe's–
Humbly accompanies, with ticks-and-tocks,
Each second that, ceaseless, repeats, rehearses
The vast world's hidden, heavenly turbulence.
I listen to the air throbbing its riddle,
Posing it endlessly; and, in the middle
Of it all, cries of birds' restless suspense...
–O heavens! Can it be that here I come–
Again, again–to live, to taste the balm
Of emptiness's dream, here in the calm
Reposing, after study's tedium!
Can I not see that, sitting, standing, lying,
Running... No matter! Man is but a dying
Creature, whom Fate pursues! Nor need she spy
On the poor living thing with prying eye:
His doom is sealed. Should he chance to know love,
Something will always burst the bonds thereof,
Be it in fearful joys' duress or peace:
Ever his tender, noble choice must cease;
He must burn, waiting, yearning fruitlessly,

Je ne vous reprends pas ma confiance innée,
Querelleuse au beau front, secrète Destinée,
Favorable aux cœurs violents!

Never to surfeit the desires that he
Begs from tomorrow... Meanwhile, I, who know
The cruelest buffetings of human woe,
Whose soul most often stands tempest-transfixed,
Who live a life midst tears and pleasures mixed,
I blame you not that I am still unbowed,
O secret Destiny, cantankerous,
You, elegant of brow, who smile on us,
    Violent of heart, unbending, proud...

"MON ESPRIT ANXIEUX..."

Mon esprit anxieux, qui n'est jamais distrait,
Vous palpe, ombre où plus rien de l'être ne subsiste,
Éternité d'avant, éternité d'après,
Double vertige autour de la vie! Et j'existe!
Et mes yeux exercés aux célestes secrets
S'enchâssent dans la nuit comme un astre. Est-il vrai
Que l'on meurt, ayant tout aimé! Que je mourrai
Sans qu'un dieu fraternel à ce moment m'assiste?
Ô ma vie, accident somptueux, vain et triste...

"ANXIOUS, MY MIND..."

Anxious, my mind, alert, will ever try
To probe you, all-consuming shade-domain,
Eternities before and after! I
Exist between your dizzinesses twain!
Star-like, embedded in the evening sky,
My eyes see all the secrets wrought on high.
What? Die despite our loves? What? I must die
Without some brother-god to ease my pain?
O life of mine, lush accident, sad, vain...

LE PLAISIR

Plaisir, le plus profond et triste mot du monde,
Qui contient tout l'espoir et contient tout l'oubli,
Qui dit l'homme exultant ou bien enseveli
Dans l'extase effrayée où les larmes abondent.

Plaisir, le seul vainqueur, pied d'airain arrêté
Sur tout effort humain. Plaisir, terme des choses,
Accostage de l'être avec l'éternité,
Plénitude, désert, ravage, immense pause;

Interrogation et reproche au destin
Pour ce ciel apparu à travers nos ténèbres,
Pour ce bref incendie enivrant, qui s'éteint
Et nous laisse sa cendre impalpable et funèbre.

Plaisir, effarement, puis révélation,
Passage de la mort franchi, clarté soudaine,
Être un dieu; connaissance, ample précision;
Puis cette pauvreté de la tendresse humaine!

Et pourtant rien ne vaut que vous, plaisir amer,
Sur qui posent le monde et tout l'humain théâtre,
Amer plaisir, profond tel la profonde mer
Qui porte allègrement les pesantes escadres!

N'est-ce pas vous toujours ces rêveuses lourdeurs
Du printemps pluvieux, ce pépiement d'eau fraîche
Dans la noire forêt, ces subites odeurs
Des bourgeons, crépitant sur les écorces rêches;
Ce cri d'oiseau avec sa tristesse de cœur
(Cri ténu et pourtant enflé comme l'orage),
Ce cri d'oiseau, le soir, n'est-ce pas votre ouvrage,
Ô sournois compagnon, solennel et moqueur,
Plaisir, vous qui toujours remplacez le bonheur!

PLEASURE

Pleasure: word most profound, sad as can be;
Word full of hope, full of forgetfulness,
Sounds that make man exult or that express
His fright, buried in tear-strewn ecstasy.

Pleasure: sole victor, foot of brass suspending,
Still, over every human striving, whence
Our being skirts the eternal, never-ending,
In fullness, void, destruction... Pause immense;

Question for fate, reproach no less... For, such
This sky-flash through the shadows, drunken bliss
That flames, burns out... And we, left but with this:
Its pyre's dead ashes that defy the touch.

Pleasure: awed fear and revelation. Then,
Passage through death, or leap, or flare... Godhead,
Knowledge precise, clearly and amply spread,
And dearth of human tenderness again!

Yet naught, O bitter pleasure, equals you,
Scene where the world acts its humanity;
Pleasure deep as the deep and bitter sea
That bears fleets' weight gaily with no to-do!

Are you not always those dream-sultrinesses
Of rain-soaked spring, that water chirping fresh
In the dark wood, the scents each bud expresses
Suddenly from the crackling bark's rough flesh;
That bird's cry, sad of heart (thin-piping sound,
Yet swelling like the storm gathering round);
Indeed, is it not yours, that night-bird cry,
O pleasure, my companion–solemn, sly–
Who would replace our happiness profound!

"LA DOULEUR EST PRESSÉE..."

La douleur est pressée et ne peut pas attendre,
Il lui faut un subit et vaste apaisement;
Je ne sais où j'ai lu ces mots plaintifs et tendres:
« Souffrir est un très long moment. »

Bondissant comme un cerf qu'un chasseur assassine,
Le turbulent désir ne peut être prudent.
C'est vous qui le criez, princesse de Racine:
« Je meurs si je vous perds, mais je meurs si j'attends.»

Ces paroles de feu, ce pantelant dilemme
Que jette à votre amant votre esprit irrité,
C'est le puissant soupir de l'être, dès qu'il aime.
– Sombre Amour, composé d'âme et de volupté,

Puisque jamais l'instant de vivre n'est propice
À ton avide espoir, prompt et vertigineux,
Puisque tout désir court vers un sûr précipice,
Et pour être éternel veut être ruineux,

Quel est donc le souhait de ces deux corps qui tremblent
Enlacés, se faisant plus serrés, plus étroits,
Comme pour se tapir dans le néant? Il semble
Qu'ils cherchent un tombeau, dans leur suave effroi.
Et la volupté n'est, peut-être, je le crois,
Que l'essai de mourir ensemble...

"SUFFERING CANNOT WAIT..."

Suffering cannot wait, brooks no delaying;
It needs a boundless and abrupt relief.
Where did I read this tender, plaintive saying:
    "Too long the moments of our grief..."?

Leaping stag that the hunter's shot lays low,
Desire knows not the wisdom of abating.
You, princess of Racine, have said it so:
"Should I lose you, I die, yet die for waiting."

Those words of fire, dilemma's breathless sighing,
Cast on your lover, whom your soul distresses,
The pant of one who loves, her passion plying...
–Love, gloom of spirit and voluptuousnesses,

Since never is life's living instant fit
For your brash hopes, impatient, dizzying;
Since every lust runs headlong toward a pit,
And, to last endless, must disaster bring;

What is the wish that, binding like a tether,
Joins tight that trembling pair–behind, before–
Huddling there in the void? Ah! Who knows whether
They seek a grave in their calm terror, or
If bliss voluptuous is nothing more
    Than the attempt to die together...

Line 8: The line is from Racine's tragedy *Andromaque,* Act III, scene 7. The present attribution notwithstanding, it is pronounced not by Andromaque but by Pyrrhus, her persistent suitor. (Trans.)

SOLITUDE

Je t'aime, mais je rêve, et mon être sans borne,
Quand le croissant des nuits montre sa belle corne,
Attiré vers les cieux par des milliers d'aimants,
S'élance, et va s'unir à tous les éléments.

Pourtant c'est toujours toi que mon désir réclame,
Mais comment pourrais-tu dominer sur mon âme,
Si tu ne peux bannir de mon cœur ébloui
Ce pouvoir d'espérer par quoi je te trahis?

SOLITUDE

I love you, but still, limitless, I dream;
And when night's crescent sports her horns, I seem
Drawn skyward by a myriad magnets hence,
Bounding, to join in all the elements.

Yet it is you I ever hunger for;
But how might you rein in my soul if your
Strength cannot rout from my heart's dazzled din
The hopefulness that lets me do you in?

TRANQUILLITÉ

Après le jour luisant d'entrain
Voici la nuit, dévote et fine,
Il semble que le ciel s'incline
Par le poids des astres sereins.
Le souffle saccadé d'un train
Transmet à la calme colline
Sa palpitation d'airain.
Dans l'ombre, les bruits qui scintillent,
- Bruits de pas, de voix, de volets -
Semblent polis comme des billes,
Comme les grains d'un chapelet.
– Ô Nuit, compatissant mystère!
Se peut-il, quand l'air est si doux
Et semble penser avec nous,
Qu'il y ait des morts dans la terre!
– Je n'ai besoin de rien ce soir
Grâce à ta tendresse amoureuse,
Une âme n'est vraiment heureuse
Que sans projets et sans espoirs.
Nous parlons sans cesse de l'âme,
Pourtant, après ce long plaisir,
Tout nous est paresse et loisir,
Plus rien en nos cœurs ne réclame;
Nous pourrions vivre ou bien mourir
Contents ainsi, calmes, à l'aise,
– Ô mon cher compagnon, serait-ce
Qu'on ne souffre que de désir?

TRANQUILLITY

Gone, now, day's dazzling energy,
And falls the night, so gentle, so
Devout. The sky seems to bow low
Beneath the stars' serenity.
A huffing train puffs fitfully
Its brassy-breathed fortissimo
Over the calm hill, pounding free.
Sounds flashing in the dark, galore–
–Shutters, steps, voices–sparks of light,
Seem like so many marbles, or
Rosary beads, smooth, polished bright.
–Night! Pact mysterious! Can it
Be–when, in tune with us, the air
Hangs soft–that there are corpses there,
In earth! Ah! I need not one whit
This night, so sweet your tenderness.
A soul is happy only when
It has no hopes, no dreams; for then,
Finished, its yearning. We profess
To plumb the soul with talk; and yet,
After life's pleasures and life's fire,
At length, no more do we require,
Nothing more need our hearts beget,
Either to covet or aspire:
Then might we live, die, peaceably.
–O dear companion, can it be
We suffer only from desire?

LA NUIT

Nuit sainte, les amants ne vous ont pas connue
Autant que les époux. C'est le mystique espoir
De ceux qui tristement s'aiment de l'aube au soir,
D'être ensemble enlacés sous votre sombre nue.

Comme un plus ténébreux et profond sacrement,
Ils convoitent cette heure interdite et secrète
Où l'animale ardeur s'avive et puis s'arrête
Dans un universel et long apaisement.

C'est le vœu le plus pur de ces pauvres complices
Dont la tendre unité ne doit pas s'avouer,
De surprendre parfois votre austère justice,
Et d'endormir parmi votre ombre protectrice
Leur amour somptueux, humble et désapprouvé...

NIGHT

O hallowed night, no lovers know your taste
As spouses do. Such is hope's mystery
For those who love from dawn to dusk: to be
Beneath your dark cloud-shadows, love-enlaced.

Like a profound and obscure sacrament,
Jealously they yearn for that secret hour
When their fleshly desires rise up and flower,
Then cease in long relief, their lust-fires spent.

Those guilty souls' purest intent, O night—
Whose tender union must ever lie hidden—
Is that your justice might assuage their plight
And that, in your protective shade, you might
Let sleep their humble love, sumptuous, forbidden...

"L'ÊTRE NE RECHERCHE..."

L'être ne recherche que soi
À travers le multiple choix
De l'amour et de ses orages.
Ô Désir, somptueux voyage
Vers notre fascinante image
Qui nous exalte ou nous déçoit!
– C'est à soi-même qu'on veut plaire
Sur le cœur brûlant qui nous plaît,
Où, dans l'ivresse et la colère,
Ne sachant si l'on aime ou hait,
Par la volupté l'on espère
Mourir, et ne mourir jamais!

"EACH BEING SEEKS BUT ITSELF..."

Each being seeks but itself, throughout
The many choices that spread out
Before it: love tempestuous...
Desire! Passionate, sumptuous
Voyage to our image of us,
That fascinates, or makes us doubt
Our worth!... It is ourselves that we
Would please as we lie, drunk, upon
His burning breast, where, blissfully–
In love? hate? anger?–we go on,
Yearning at once to die, yet be
Alive forever and anon!

“NI L’ÉBLOUISSEMENT DU REGARD...”

Ni l’éblouissement du regard qui reçoit
L’aurore, l’horizon et les coteaux sur soi;
Ni les vergers avec leurs tentures de pêches,
Ni le ciel pur par qui la chaleur semble fraîche,
Ni le subit bonheur d’un noir oiseau, cloué
D’extase, semble-t-il, sur l’azur large et tendre,
Ne valent la douceur de ce que peut entendre
Daphnis se reposant sur le cœur de Chloé....

"NEITHER THE DAZZLING DAWN..."

Neither the dazzling dawn beyond the high
And distant hills, falling upon the eye;
Nor orchards hung with peaches; nor the fair,
Pure sky that seems to cool the torrid air;
Nor, soaring on the azure's tenderest
Expanse, a black bird's sudden ecstasy,
Can match the sweet bliss Daphnis knows when he
Reposes, calm, upon his Chloe's breast...

Lines 7-8: Daphnis and Chloé are the love-struck pastoral heroes of a second-century C.E. romance, ascribed to one Longus, though not without reservations. They have come down to more recent times as embodiments of their genre, inspiring a number of popular works not the least important of which was the 1912 ballet commissioned by Diaghilev and choreographed by Fokine, to music by Maurice Ravel. (Trans.)

POÈME DE L'AMOUR

(1927)

I

Ce fut long, difficile et triste
De te révéler ma tendresse;
La voix s'élance et puis résiste,
La fierté succombe et se blesse.

Je ne sais vraiment pas comment
J'ai pu t'avouer mon amour;
J'ai craint l'ombre et l'étonnement
De ton bel œil couleur du jour.

Je t'ai porté cette nouvelle!
Je t'ai tout dit! je m'y résigne;

Et tout de même, comme un cygne,
Je mets ma tête sous mon aile...

I

How long it took, how sad it was
How hard, to tell you of my love;
The voice begins, then hems and haws...
Pride falls and bears the woes thereof.

Truly, I know not how I could
Tell you my love, find words to say;
I feared lest you, astounded, would
Dim dark your eye, hued fair as day.

But still I told you everything!
But still, confessed... Ah, so it goes;

And yet, in timid, swan-like pose
I stand, head tucked beneath my wing...

II

Comprends que je déraisonne,
Que mon cœur, avec effroi,
Dans tout l'espace tâtonne
Sans se plaire en nul endroit...

Je n'ai besoin que de toi
Qui n'as besoin de personne!

II

Listen how I rave, undone,
How my fearful heart, askew,
Looks for pleasure, finding none,
Though it grope the whole world through...

You alone I need; and you
Have no need of anyone!

X

Dans les ténèbres de Vérone
On entend mourir Juliette.
À Venise, - ardente, inquiète,
On voit suffoquer Desdémone.

– Envions le cœur qui s'arrête
Quand un excès d'amour l'étonne!
Le plaisir n'est que ce qu'on prête,
Mais la vie est ce que l'on donne...

X

Verona's shades as dusk descends:
Hear Juliet sigh her dying day...
Venice unstrung–see lust's display:
Desdémona her last breath spends...

–Yearn we for that heartbeat that ends
When loves excesses awe, dismay!
Pleasure is what one only lends,
Life it is that one gives away...

Lines 3-4: It is ambiguous in the original whether the adjectives refer to Venice or to Desdemona. I try to skirt the problem. (Trans.)

XI

Lorsque je souffre trop de ton brillant visage,
Quand mon cœur asservi ne peut plus te quitter,
Je songe qu'autrefois de lointains paysages,
Des ports et leurs vaisseaux, de fameuses cités
M'éblouissaient ainsi; mon désir irrité
Croyait ne pas pouvoir vivre sans ces rivages...

– Je n'en eus plus besoin quand je les eus chantés.

XI

When your charms shine so brightly that, among them
My suffering heart must bide, on many a shore
Far-flung I muse, lands that I knew before,
Whose towns, ports, boats dazzled my thoughts, unstrung them,
Pricked my desire, convinced me more and more
I needed them to bear the life I bore...

—No more I needed them once I had sung them.

XVIII

Quand la musique en feu déchaîne ses poèmes,
Quand ce noble ouragan soulève jusqu'aux cieux
Les désirs empourprés des cœurs ambitieux,
Sachant ton humble vie, et sa faiblesse même,
Moi, toujours simplement et pauvrement je t'aime...

XVIII

When music's fires unleash their poetry,
And when its noble gales blow to the skies
The crimsoned longings of hearts on the rise,
Knowing how humble, frail your life can be,
Myself, I love you gently, modestly...

XXV

Le silence répand son vide;
Le ciel, lourd d'orage, est houleux;
On voit bouger, tiède et limpide,
Le vent dans un mimosa bleu.

Prolongeant sa douceur étale,
Le jour ressemble aux autres jours;
Un craintif et secret amour
Rêve, sans ouvrir ses pétales.

– Ainsi, pour longtemps en jouir,
La Hollande, en ses vastes serres,
Par des blocs de glace resserre
Les tulipes qui vont s'ouvrir...

XXV

Silence spreads wide its emptiness;
The storm-hung sky waves like the tide.
In the clear breeze's warm caress,
Sway blue mimosas side to side.

Day, soft-becalmed, long as it might,
Delays, like other days, its start.
A secret love, timid of heart,
Dreams, with its petals still closed tight.

–Just so, in Dutch greenhouses vast,
Tulips in blocks of ice will be
Enclosed, to make their pleasure last,
Whose petals will, one day, bloom free...

XXVIII

On m'a parlé ce soir des villes savoureuses
Qui sur les mers du Sud rêvent indolemment,
Répandant leur odeur de rose et de piment,
Sans connaitre leur prix, sans se savoir heureuses!

Tu ressembles souvent, dans ton charme attristé,
À l'ignorant bonheur de ces rêveuses villes,
Toi qui fais émaner la chaude volupté
De ton être évasif, distrait, triste et tranquille...

XXVIII

They spoke to me of towns lush, motionless,
Spreading their rose-and-pepper scents about,
Lazing in South Seas' indolence, without
An inkling of their priceless happiness!

Often, your own sad charm is much like this
Mindless contentment of those cities dreaming,
You, from whose very being wafts passion's bliss–
Your being so calm, so vaguely wistful-seeming.

XXXV

Es-tu bon? Oui, puisque je t'aime
Et que tu vis. Je puis tenir
Tout acquiescement de toi-même:
L'amour n'a pas d'autre problème
Que d'autoriser le désir...

XXXV

Are you good? Yes, I know, for I
Love you and you live on. You need
Grant me no other leave thereby.
Love's only aim: to justify
Desire's demands, duly decreed...

XL

Aimer, c'est de ne mentir plus.
Nulle ruse n'est nécessaire
Quand le bras chaleureux enserre
Le corps fuyant qui nous a plu.

– Crois à ma voix qui réve et chante
Et qui construit ton paradis.
Saurais-tu que je suis méchante
Si je ne te l'avais pas dit?

– Faiblement méchante, en pensée,
Et pour retrouver par moment
Cette solitude sensée
Que j'ai reniée en t'aimant!

XL

To love is to stop lying; thus
No need for falsehood or deceit
To hug the fleeing body, meet
To please our passion amorous.

Trust in my voice that dreams and sings,
And builds for you a paradise.
Didn't I say–midst other things!–
That I'm not really very nice?

Not nice at all–though in my head–
Trying to find, a time or two,
That solitude wise-judgmented,
That I gave up in loving you!

XLV

Ceux qui, hors du rêve et des transes
Par quoi le souffle est empêché,
Goûtent d'heureuses impudences,
Semblent par le sort protégés.
Nul dieu jaloux n'est attaché
À punir leur insouciance,

– Et peut-être que la souffrance
Est l'unique et sombre péché.

XLV

Those who—except in dream or trance
That make one, struggling, gasp for air—
Enjoy their little deeds askance,
Seem fate-protected, devil-may-care.
No jealous god has eager been
To punish their insouciant stance,

—Suffering pain may be, perchance,
The one and only darkest sin.

XLIX

On est bon si l'on est tranquille,
Content, indifférent, distrait;
Mais si, plié sur son secret,
L'esprit sent sa force servile,
Qui dira l'ardeur, la bonté,
D'un instant de méchanceté?

XLIX

One is good if one is content,
Calm, and indifferent, lost in thought;
But if, firm on its secret bent,
Mind's efforts are a slavish lot,
Who can the fire, the good express
From one moment of nastiness?

LIV

Quand un soudain sommeil a séparé de toi
Ma pensée attentive, anxieuse et tenace;
Quand je suis prisonnière en ce cachot étroit,
Et quand l'amour, toujours pareil à la menace,

Semble avoir dans le songe égaré les contours
De ton être par qui me parvient l'atmosphère,
Je goûte obscurément cet instant calme et court
Dont s'est enfui le mal que ton œil peut me faire...

LIV

When sudden sleep severs you from my thought,
Anxious, attentive, and unyielding; when
I am a prisoner in this cell, tight-wrought;
And when love, menace-like, seems threatening then

To spirit off to dreams your flesh-curved lines–
Their atmosphere that hovers round me, through me–
I taste that calm, brief moment's dark designs,
Free of the mischief that your eye can do me...

LVII

Enfin la première nuit froide!
Plus de vents dansants, amollis.
L'atmosphère est tendue et roide,
Le beau ciel d'argent dépoli
Allonge sa paix où se creuse
Le puits des étoiles neigeuses.
– Va-t-il enfin me protéger,
Ce climat soudain sans tendresse,
De ton beau visage étranger
Sur lequel mon amour s'abaisse
Comme ces œillets las, déteints,
Qu'englobent les pleurs du matin?...

LVII

At last, the season's first cold night!
Now no more softly dancing breezes.
The atmosphere is crisp and tight,
The sky, a silver gray, appeases
Space with its peace, where we see rise
The deep well of the snow-starred skies.
Will it protect me, finally–
This climate suddenly unkind–
From your sweet face, foreign to me,
Whereon my love grovels, resigned,
Like dreams dull, weary, self-abasing,
That morning's tears enclose, embracing?...

LVIII

J'ai puissamment goûté l'orgueil
D'avoir reçu de la nature
L'éclat bondissant d'un bel œil,
Archer double de la figure;

J'ai souvent, devant des miroirs,
Ressenti la force contente
De m'arrêter, d'apercevoir
Une héroïne palpitante;

Mais combien faible est la valeur
D'un visage pur et vainqueur,

Alors que je t'offre un tel cœur?

LVIII

How staunchly have I taken pride
In nature's boons, when I behold
My fair expression, flashing-eyed,
Darts of a double-bowman bold;

Contented have I oft-times been,
By mirrors poised, to gaze upon
My image strong, contained therein,
Of palpitating paragon.

But weak my beauty's virtues few:
Triumphant, proud... what can they do

When this poor heart I offer you!

Line 8: Translators are faced with choices as often as creative writers. It was hard for me to decide between two versions of the first two stanzas of this bagatelle. Rather than trash the one unused, I append it here so that the reader can decide on the wisdom of my choice, or lack of it. (Trans.)

Great pride have I felt in the prize
By nature wrought: face that entrances,
Flashing a pair of sparkling eyes—
Bowmen twain, casting arrow-glances.

Before the mirror, frequently,
I stand and gaze in happy mood
As the fair heroine I see
In her heart-throbbing pulchritude!

LIX

Tu sais, je n'étais pas modeste,
Je n'ignorais pas les sommets
Où je vivais, puissante, agreste,
Rêveuse, universelle, - mais

J'ai soudain vu sur ton visage
Un clair et vivant paysage,
Où, morne, insensible, lassé,
Tu m'as défendu de passer...

LIX

You know, I was not modest; no,
I knew my strengths, my dreams, and what
Summits I haunted here below:
A country lass and worldly—but

I looked upon your face, and there
I saw a living landscape, where,
Weary, unfeeling, somber, you
Would not permit me to pass through...

LXVII

Moi seule je connais ta langoureuse allure,
Tous les autres regards peuvent bien s'y tromper.
Mais j'ai surpris (ô juin, par l'orage estompé!)
Comme un cristal où gît l'invisible fêlure,
Ton rire épanoui, d'angoisse entrecoupé...

LXVII

I alone know your languorous manner, fit
But for my eyes: others' would ill judge you.
I've caught your laugh (O June storm-muted!); it
Crackles like crystal flaw, like subtle split
Unseen... Vast laugh, with anguished gasps run through...

LXIX

Si vraiment les mots t'embarrassent,
Ne dis rien. Rêve. N'aie pas froid;
C'est moi qui parle et qui t'embrasse;
Laisse-moi répandre sur toi,
Comme le doux vent dans les bois,
Ce murmure immense, à voix basse...

LXIX

If words put you too ill at ease,
Say nothing. Dream. But be not cold.
Let me speak, me, who kiss you, hold
You in my arms; like woodland breeze
That murmurs low, let me enfold
You in great whispers, hushed, like these...

LXXI

Il fut un temps où, turbulente...
Sous les yeux des astres divins,
Grave, ignorant que tout est vain,
J'exigeais de rester vivante.

Aujourd'hui j'aspire au début
D'une éternelle somnolence,
Morte mille fois d'avoir bu
Tous les poisons dans ton silence...

LXXI

Time was, tempestuous, I would strive–
As stars divine gazed limitless,
Unmindful of life's emptiness–
Stubbornly but to stay alive.

Today I yearn to let begin,
At last, an everlasting sleep,
Dead myriad times from drinking in
The poisons of your silence deep...

LXXVI

Combien de fois aurais-je dû
Me sentir lasse et sans courage!
Mais mon cœur n'a jamais perdu
Son désir pour ton beau visage.

Dans mon puissant amour tu n'as
Vu que ma douceur de colombe;
Pourtant je veux que sur ma tombe
L'on inscrive: Elle s'obstina...

LXXVI

Though many a time I might have been
Weary, undone, without a trace
Of strength, yet did my heart, done in,
Still yearn to see your lovely face.

My rugged love showed you one side–
Only my dove-soft sweetness; but
Upon my gravestone this is what
I would they write: "Stubborn, she tried..."

LXXXIII

Tu vis, - moi je porte le faix
De ton étrange et dur destin,
Puisque le mal que tu me fais
Tu ne peux pas en être atteint!

LXXXIII

You live, but I bear more than you
The weight of your strange destiny;
For never can you suffer too
All the pain that you do to me!

LXXXVI

Aucun jour je ne me suis dit
Que tu pouvais être mortel.
Tu ressembles au paradis,
À tout ce qu'on croit éternel!
– Mais, ce soir, j'ai senti, dans l'air
Humide d'un parc triste et blême,
La terreuse odeur des asters
Et du languissant chrysanthème...

Quoi! tu peux mourir! – et je t'aime!

LXXXVI

Never has it occurred to me
That you are a mere mortal... Never!
Paradise-like, you seem to be
Something one thinks will last forever!
–But tonight I smelled in the air–
Moist–of a park drear to the eye,
Asters' earthy perfume, and there,
Chrysanthemums', lolling nearby...

What? I love you! –And you can die!

XCVIII

En ton absence je ne puis
Être plus ou moins seule. Aucune
Voix qui console, aucun appui
N'atténuerait mon infortune;

Il faudrait qu'un autre être soit,
Qu'il brille à mes yeux! qu'il s'oppose
À ton image, à tes exploits!
Mais pourquoi l'espérer? Pourquoi?
– Implacable métamorphose,
Dans mon esprit actif, adroit,
C'est toi seul qui redeviens toi!

XCVIII

Without you too much goes amiss:
I cannot be alone. For me,
No pitying voice, no sympathy,
To calm me in woe's drear abyss;

Another you would have to be
The one held dear, to shine before
My eyes, assuming bodily
Your deeds, your image, even your
Very self!... But why hope for this?
–Resistless metamorphosis,
My mind, unerring monitor,
Turns you to you alone once more!

Line 12: I've seen fit to take liberties with the poet's rhyme scheme, no less capricious than mine and which corresponds to no particular form. (Trans.)

XCIX

Un triste orgue de Barbarie
Enfonce dans l'air du matin,
Comme à coups de couteau qui crie,
Un vulgaire, un pointu refrain,

Et même cela, cela même,
Ce triste chant malade et maigre,
Dans la rue où souffle un vent aigre,
Me fait songer au bleu foyer
De ton regard droit et noyé,
Et m'indique combien je t'aime!

XCIX

A hurdy-gurdy's plaintive twang
Stabs, dagger-like, the morning breeze;
Sharp-pointed notes clatter and clang
Their vulgar, prickly melodies.

But even that—ah yes, that too!—
That sad song, sickly and effete,
Over the bitter-windblown street,
Makes me dream of the blue expanse
Of your faraway, honest glance,
And makes clear all my love for you!

CV

Sauf toi, tous les humains regards
Peuvent s'assurer de ma peine;
Loin de toi, je gis, l'œil hagard,
Sans voix, et respirant à, peine.

Que fais-tu, toi qui n'es aimé
Que de moi seule avec extase?
Saurai-je desceller le vase
De ton beau sourire fermé?

Se peut-il qu'il soit admissible
Quand tout dans l'amour est possible
Que je périsse de désir?
– Bel être qu'on ne peut saisir,
Âme ferme, calme, têtue,
Confiante en des lendemains,
Lorsque, moi, chaque heure me tue,
Pourquoi ne pas tendre ta main
À ma main qui, rien qu'en touchant
Ton poignet nonchalant et triste,
M'indiquerait pourquoi j'existe,
Et me restituerait mon chant!...

CV

Save your own, every human eye
Witnesses my pain, succorless;
Far from your side, wide-eyed I lie,
Scarce breathing, speechless my distress...

You who are loved ecstatically
By me alone... What do you do?
Will I break free the smile that you
Seal, like a lovely vase, from me?

When love allows of everything,
Can it be that my cherishing
Will do me in? –O you, fair swain,
Whom one would clutch, alas, in vain,
Calm, solid, headstrong soul that stands
Confident in all its tomorrows,
Why will you not reach out your hands
To mine, amidst my murderous sorrows;
I, whom the slightest touch upon
The languid, sad curve of your wrist,
Would tell at last why I exist
And would restore my song, long gone!...

CX

Sans doute ma vie est plus morne,
Et plus stable aussi qu'autrefois.
Ce n'est plus l'espace sans borne
Que je poursuis; j'assiste à toi.

Mais tandis que mes pas s'arrêtent
Auprès de ton cœur grave et sûr,
Des dieux offensés me regrettent
À quelque banquet de l'azur!

CX

My life seems duller, I confess,
Than once it was, more staid withal.
I seek no boundless, limitless
Expanse of space; you are my all.

And yet, though I stray not from this
Grave heart of yours, so solid, stable,
Banqueting gods, offended, miss
My presence at their azure table!

CXIX

Le bonheur ainsi que l'ennui,
Comme deux fleuves dans la nuit,
S'en vont, rêveurs et téméraires,
Se perdre dans les eaux amères.

– Pourquoi nous semble-t-il toujours,
Dans la peine ou bien dans l'amour,
Qu'aucun des deux n'est éphémère?...

CXIX

Happiness and chagrin, like two
Rivers that stream night's darkness through–
Dreaming, daring–course on till they
Join in life's acrid waterway.

Why does it always seem to us,
Be we loving or dolorous,
That neither one lasts but a day?...

CXXVII

Les cœurs purs et spirituels
Ne possèdent qu'un froid atome
Dont le fragile et faible baume
N'est ni divin ni sensuel.

Mais dans sa force qui réclame,
Dans son miracle de chaleur,
De raison, de fièvre, de pleurs,
Le corps seul témoigne pour l'âme...

CXXVII

Hearts pure that ply their soul to us
Possess a fragrance cold and calm,
Whose powerless and fragile balm
Is nor divine nor sensuous.

But in its strength, hearty and whole,
The body–miracle of heat,
With fever, reason, tears replete–
Alone bears witness to the soul...

CXXXII

C'est d'une adresse humble et savante
De t'avoir aimé de la sorte,
Car, par mon cœur qui se transporte
En ta force heureuse et mouvante,
Je ne vis plus d'être vivante,
Et ne mourrai pas d'être morte!

CXXXII

Clever the way I loved you! For–
Humble, wise–though my heart would bide
Within your sprightliness, inside
That store of strength you gaily bore,
I live no more for living, nor
Shall I be dead for having died!

CLX

Que puis-je te donner qui te rende paisible?
Puis-je chercher pour toi, aux cieux inaccessibles,
    Les étoiles, jouets des anges?
Verrai-je ton regard devenir clair et doux,
Cependant que tes mains aux rêveuses phalanges
Reposent noblement sur tes calmes genoux?...

CLX

What might I give you that will calm your mood?
Can I fetch, in that reachless multitude,
    The angels' plaything-stars? Would I
See your glance, soft and bright, mayhap
Grow sweeter as your dream-hands, by the by,
Rest nobly in the calmness of your lap?...

CLXIII

J'ai vraiment vécu des jours tels,
Si longs, si lourds par la souffrance,
Que je songe avec complaisance
Que rien d'humain n'est immortel!

N'être plus! ni moi, ni toi-même!
Oui, ni toi! par qui j'ai connu
L'horreur de craindre ce qu'on aime!
– Ignorer combien tu m'as plu,
Et que tu fus l'homme suprême
Par qui tout autre était exclu,

– Toi dont j'ai baisé le bras nu!...

CLXIII

So long the many days that I
Have lived, heavy with suffering,
That now I muse, unquestioning,
That nothing human but must die!

To be no more! Nor me, nor you!
Yes, even you, who taught me this
Fear of the hurt such love can do!
—How great my love? I scarcely knew
How much—O paragon of bliss!—
Your love cast out all others too,

—You, on whose arm I placed a kiss!...

CLXIV

Meurt-on d'aimer? On peut le croire,
Tant c'est une mortelle histoire!

– Pourtant il me reste toujours
La grâce, au loin, de tes contours.
– Et la douleur dont tu m'enivres,
Dont je crois que je vais mourir,
Est peut-être, ô prudent désir!
Le seul secret qui me fait vivre...

CLXIV

Does love kill? Can one die of love?
So it seems, such death's woe thereof!
–And yet, though distant, still are mine
Your body's grace, its every line.
–And the bliss of the pain you give,
Enough to make me drunk and die,
May the one secret be, whereby–
O lust reined in!–I yet may live...

CLXXV

Rien; l'univers n'est rien. Nulle énigme pour l'homme
Dont l'esprit et les sens ont perçu le néant.
– La turbulente vie hasardeuse, et le somme
À jamais, dans le sol maussade et dévorant!

Rien! Partout l'éphémère et partout le risible,
Partout l'insulte au cœur, partout la surdité
Du Destin, qui choisit pour délicate cible
La noblesse de l'homme et sa sécurité.

– Et parmi cette affreuse et poignardante injure,
Seulement toi, visage au masque de velours,
Divinité maligne, enivrante, âpre et pure,
Consolateur cruel, doux et terrible Amour!

1920 - 1923

CLXXV

Nothing, the universe! For one whose sense
And spirit pierce its puzzle meaningless,
No charade! Life? Turbulent accidents...
Glum earth: sleep's all-devouring endlessness!

Nothing! The laughable, transience confected
Everywhere, heart's offense, and Destiny
Turning deaf ear to man, left unprotected,
Casting its darts on his nobility.

–And amid all that torment deadly-bladed,
You alone, velvet-cheeked masked god, source of
Drunk passion, sweet and bitter, pure and jaded,
Wanton and mild... You, cruel consoler: Love!

1920 - 1923

L'HONNEUR DE SOUFFRIR

(1927)

II

Ainsi la vie ample et savante,
L'exaltante splendeur des cieux,
Nos regards qui jouaient entre eux,
Notre loyauté, ma constante
Tendresse, mon cœur soucieux
De toi, dont j'étais dépendante,
- Puisque tu me laisses vivante
Alors que se sont clos tes yeux, -

Ce n'était donc pas sérieux!

II

Life in its wisdom, its largess,
The heavens in their splendor spread,
Our glances' play, gay-spirited,
Our loyalty, my tenderness
Unbending, my heart surfeited
With care for you, my all, no less...
–Since you leave me alive, though dead
Your sightless eyes shut tight... Ah yes–

It was all just a joke I guess!

V

Morts qui me fûtes chers, ne soyez pas jaloux,
Votre cendreuse voix me séduit et m'appelle,
Je suis encore avec les anges sur l'échelle,
Je n'ai pas pu venir si vite auprès de vous,
Mais je chancelle.

Comme la lune joue avec les flots des mers
Et mène l'océan de l'une à l'autre rive,
Mon souffle est retenu parmi les choses vives,
Je n'ai pas encor pu me dérober à l'air,
Pourtant j'arrive...

V

Dear dead souls, be not jealous of me, pray;
Seductive, ashen-voiced you call to me.
Climbing the angel-ladder, I must be
Ever behind you, as I make my way,
Falteringly.

As moonbeams frolic with the waves until
They lead the tide from shore to shore, here, there;
I have not yet learned to escape the air–
Living things bind my breath about them still–
But soon I will...

VI

Ils ont inventé l'âme afin que l'on abaisse
Le corps, unique lieu de rêve et de raison,
Asile du désir, de l'image et des sons,
Et par qui tout est mort dès le moment qu'il cesse.

Ils nous imposent l'âme, afin que lâchement
On détourne les yeux du sol, et qu'on oublie,
Après l'injurieux ensevelissement,
Que sous le vin vivant tout est funèbre lie.
- Je ne commettrai pas envers votre bonté,
Envers votre grandeur, secrète mais charnelle,
Ô corps désagrégés, ô confuses prunelles,
La trahison de croire à votre éternité.
Je refuse l'espoir, l'altitude, les ailes,
Mais étrangère au monde et souhaitant le froid
De vos affreux tombeaux, trop bas et trop étroits,
J'affirme, en recherchant vos nuits vastes et vaines,
Qu'il n'est rien qui survive à la chaleur des veines!

VI

The soul is an invention that they wrought
To scorn the body, which, alone, gives rise
To reason, dream, sight, sound, desire; where dies
Everything, when death wastes the flesh to naught.

They press the soul upon us so that we
May turn our craven eyes from earth, when done
Entombment's foul offense; and so that one
May forget that life's wine leaves but death's lee.
"O bodies worn apart, O shadow-gaze,
I'll not betray your hidden fleshly grace
With a faith in some deathless resting-place
Of life eternal, to the end of days!
I spurn hope's wingèd flights to lofty space!
Yet, alien to this world, I seek death's chill
And strait, too distant grave; and, yearning still,
I vow, craving your night—vast, vain, effete—
That naught lives past your veins' blood-pulsing heat.

VII

Ébloui, pur, minutieux,
Le regard fixé sur ma vie,
Vous avez déroulé les cieux
Sur la route que j'ai suivie.

L'esprit sagace, prompt, actif,
Quand je défaillais de moi-même,
Votre voix rendait mon cœur vif.
Vous m'apprîtes jusqu'où l'on aime!

Par votre amour tout était franc
Et moins lourd dans ma destinée...
– C'est un soir d'automne, en mourant,
Que vous m'avez assassinée.

VII

Dazzled, precise, pristine the gaze
You cast upon my life; you spread
The heavens unfurled over my days,
Over the road I chose to tread.

Quick-witted, spirit keen... But when
Weaker I chanced at length to grow,
Your voice livened my heart again:
You taught me how far love could go!

Your love made everything fresh, pure,
Unburdening my destiny...
—One autumn eve you died, and your
Death it is that has murdered me.

X

Nul lit, nulle chambre, nul toit
N'affaibliront mon épouvante
Que tu sois mort et moi vivante.

– Dans le sol noir, étroit et froid,
J'ai un rendez-vous avec toi!

X

No bed, no chamber ceiling will
Lighten my fear as muse I do
That you lie dead and I live still.

—In earth-space narrow, dark, and chill,
I have a rendezvous with you!

XIV

Vivre, permanente surprise!
L'amour de soi, quoi que l'on dise!
L'effort d'être, toujours plus haut,
Le premier parmi les égaux,
La vanité pour le visage,
Pour la main, le sein, le genou,
Tout le tendre humain paysage!
L'orgueil que nous avons de nous,
Secrètement. L'honneur physique,
Cette intérieure musique
Par quoi nous nous guidons, et puis
Le sol creux, les cordes, le puits
Où lourdement va disparaître
Le corps ivre d'éternité.

– Et l'injure de cesser d'être,
Pire que n'avoir pas été!

XIV

Life, permanent surprise! Self-love,
Say what you will! To rise above,
Strive to rise higher, ever higher,
First among equals, vain desire
To best the human landscape: breast,
And face, and knee, and hand—whatever!
All of them, each the tenderest!
The vanity we feel, but never
Dare to express. Our body's pride,
Honor, a music deep inside,
Guiding our steps, driving us on,
And then, the empty sod, anon,
The cords, the body lowered in,
Soon gone, drunk on eternity.

—And, worse than having never been,
The curse of ceasing now to be.

XVII

Chaque être souffrant seul croit qu'il a l'apanage
D'un mal plus singulier, plus sombre et plus cuisant.
Il connaît les combats mystérieux du sang
Contre l'esprit armé de son amer courage.

Mais, ayant plus vécu, je me meurs davantage...

XVII

Each suffering creature thinks that he, before
All others, feels woe's sole and darkmost sting.
He knows blood's brave, mysterious parrying
Against the spirit, bitter-armed for war.

But, having longer lived, I die still more...

XVIII

Rien ne me touche plus, je me sens morte aussi.
Mon aride tristesse ignore les soucis.
Tu m'aimais, toute chose est avec toi finie.
Mon plaisir fut ton but. Que t'importent mes pleurs
Tu ne connaîtras pas ma penchante agonie!
– Sachant que tout est vain, et surtout la douleur,
Je n'ai pas même mis sur ta tombe une fleur…

XVIII

Nothing can touch me now, dead I feel too.
My arid grief ignores life's dread to-do.
My pleasure was your all, for you loved me,
But you are gone and all is done. My weeping
Will matter not to you. You will not see
The tears I shed, nor know my agony.
–All is in vain, and pain defies its keeping.
I even placed no flower where you lie sleeping...

XX

Cela fut, et puis disparaît,
Et jamais rien ne se remplace.
Je le sais tant, que je suis lasse
D'être un univers de regret

Je cherche en vain l'oubli, l'espoir, l'inconscience,
Pour être délivrée enfin de ton absence!

XX

It was, never to be returning,
Disappeared in eternity.
I know: how weary, I, to be
A universe of loss and yearning!

Vain, I seek mindless hope, forgetfulness,
To be freed from your absence comfortless!

XXVII

Des cœurs furent heureux le jour où tu es né.
Et pourtant le présent, plaintif ou fortuné,
Est un flot bref, rompu par le temps qui s'écoule.
– Une foule animée est une morte foule
Pour le regard précis vers le futur tourné.

– Le vif et l'actuel sont de puissants mensonges,
Puisque tout ce qui germe, éclôt et se prolonge,
Dans l'infini cruel est déjà terminé!

XXVII

Hearts rejoiced at your birth. But, be it said,
The present–joyous or dour-spirited–
Is a brief stream that passing time cuts through.
–A lively-thronging flood throngs dead into
Whoever toward the future turns his head.
–The here-and-now, the living, are but lies,
Since everything that buds, blooms, ramifies,
In the cruel infinite, is long since dead!

XXXIV

Il convient que l'on appelle âme
Cet excès de feu, de couleurs,
Dont la jeunesse se réclame.
– Mais quand l'arbre perdra ses fleurs,
Il faudra bien qu'un jour tu rames
Sur la galère du malheur.

C'est le corps qui verse les pleurs!

XXXIV

We call it "soul"—and well we do—
That flaming, many-hued excess
Of passion that youth lays claim to.
—But when the trees stand flowerless,
A galley-slave, one day, will you
Row with your woeful oar. Ah yes!

Flesh, not the soul, weeps its distress!

XXXV

Le jour, hymne silencieux,
Dans sa pure et limpide essence
Entrouvre à toute connaissance
Le vide consolant des cieux.

Nul voile, en ce feu bleu d'été,
Ne peut tromper la créature,
Ni masquer la simplicité
De l'inconsciente nature.

– Mais je ne fais aucun accueil
À la volupté du ciel calme.
Je ne vois ni roses ni palmes.

La beauté du monde est dans l'œil.

XXXV

Light, day's hymn, silent exultation
In limpid essence exquisite,
Lets glimpse each conscious mind a bit
Of heavens' empty consolation.

No sail against the fiery blue
Gulls man with summer folderol,
Or masks the simple fact, too true,
That nature knows no pain at all.

–Yet, blissful though the tranquil sky,
I ply no welcome debonair.
No palms, no roses see I there.

World's beauty looms but in the eye.

XXXVIII

Naïvement, innocemment,
Non par fierté mais par faiblesse,
Révérant votre assentiment,
J'ai connu l'orgueil des déesses.

Puis soudain vos yeux, votre voix,
Pour la mort m'ont abandonnée.
J'ai délaissé ma destinée
Et je succombe autour de moi.

– Pureté, opulence, emblème,
Tant de rêve compose un lis!
Je n'aurais jamais cru, jadis,
Que l'on était si peu soi-même...

XXXVIII

Naïve, artlessly innocent–
Not proudly, but with weakness's
Reverence for your heart's content–
I know the pride of goddesses.

Then, suddenly, your voice, your eyes,
Abandon me for death's domain.
I leave me fate there, where it lies,
And round about yield to my pain.

Purity, emblem, power and pelf...
Lily, dream-symbol, death-sign wrought!
Never before would I have thought
That one so little was oneself...

XLI

J'ai connu la fiévreuse et mordante détresse;
La stupeur; le lointain des couleurs et des bruits
Qui n'enveloppent plus un corps plein de paresse.

– À présent, enfoncée en quelque étrange nuit,
J'oppose pesamment au destin qui me nuit
Le pur désert d'un cœur où la révolte cesse,
Et la sérénité, plus lasse que l'ennui!...

XLI

I knew the feverish, biting distress,
The stupor; distant-hued cacophony
That swathes no more a body's idleness.

—Now, plunged deep in a strange night, ponderously
I pit against the fate that harries me
A heart's pure, barren void, grown struggleless—
A calm serene, more weary than ennui!

XLV

J'aurais pu ne jamais connaître
Le dur besoin de ne plus être.
Mais puisque à jamais tu te tais,
Puisque se sont défaits tes yeux,
Je songe d'un cœur radieux
Au néant qui m'épouvantait.
– Car ma peur de mourir, c'était
L'angoisse de te dire adieu…

XLV

That life must cruelly cease to be
Might have remained unknown to me.
But since forever now death draws
You to its silence, blind of eye,
Radiant, my heart need not defy
The nothingness I feared; because
If death anguished my thoughts, it was
The pain of telling you good-bye...

LI

Les morts qui m'ont aimée ont vaincu ta beauté,
Passant, subit ami révélé, frère étrange,
Beau regard rudoyant et pur, tristesse d'ange,
Azur humain pesant sur mon cœur tourmenté!

Quoi! quand la créature est chaque jour flétrie,
Quand le corps, même net, brillant et vigoureux,
N'est, dans le jeu voilé des tissus ténébreux,
Qu'une secrète, enclose et vague boucherie,

Tu m'apparus soudain suave et ravissant,
Composé par le miel, l'astre, la tubéreuse.
Plus que le suc des fleurs j'ai révéré ton sang,
Ta grâce m'accablait et me rendait peureuse.

– Et quelquefois encor, si lasse que je sois,
Si livrée au pouvoir des funèbres tempêtes,
Ta rêveuse clarté me fait baisser la tête,
Et mon désir m'enivre autant qu'il me déçoit!

LI

Those dead who loved me laid your beauty low,
O fair glance—brash, pure, angel-sad, divine:
Passerby, sudden friend, strange brother mine,
Azure-turned-man, weighting my heart with woe!

What! When, each day, she—creature unrevealed
Amid the flesh's vigor, sharp and clear—
Withers in shadowed warp and woof, a mere
Vaguely enclosed, clandestine killing-field,

Lo! Soft-spellbinding, you would rise up, looming,
Of dog-rose, honey, star-shine fair arrayed.
More I revered your blood than nectar blooming,
Your grace beset me, and I stood afraid.

But, still, at times—weary, spent though I be,
And in thrall to harsh tempests of the dead—
Clear as a dream, your sight bows low my head;
Lust makes me drunk yet disillusions me!

LII

Le monde épars s'agrège, et d'un doux mouvement
Met sa force et sa joie au profit des amants;
Leur ivresse, soudain, sent se détourner d'elle
La persécution de la mort éternelle.
Un mystère ingénu, et qui semble fidèle,
Protège puissamment le rivage des lits.
– Mais si l'on songe au net et magnifique oubli
Qui sur la volupté lentement s'établit;
Si l'on songe à la paix dolente qui recouvre
Cet abîme d'azur que le désir entr'ouvre,
Est-il vraiment suprême, auguste et suffisant
Le misérable amour dont s'enivre le sang?

LII

The world disjointed gently joins again,
Casting its strength and joy on love's domain;
All at once lovers sense their drunkenness
Freed from a stalking death's timeless duress.
A mystery naïve–faithful no less–
Staunchly defends the borders of the bed.
–But when we muse on how the ponderous tread
Of splendid, pure forgetfulness will spread
Over that bliss; how peaceful pain shrouds too
Azure's abyss, though lust come poking through,
Is love truly august, supreme? That vain,
Poor, drunken love, whose blood befogs the brain?

LIV

Silence, mouvement, arpège,
Toute douceur est dans tes os!
Sous mon regard qui te protège
De son poétique réseau,
Tu te poses comme la neige
Et t'élèves comme l'oiseau!

LIV

Silence, movement, arpeggio-sound...
Your bones with every sweetness ring!
In my protecting glance wrapped round
With web of poem-covering,
You lie like snow upon the ground,
But like a bird rise and take wing!

LVI

Je crois voir, entendre, - mais rien
De terrestre, d'aérien,
Ne me touche, ne m'intéresse,
N'éveille ma morne paresse,
Qu'en montrant à mon triste esprit,
- Et fût-ce une cloche qui sonne,
Un passant, une odeur, un cri, -
L'arabesque de ta personne...

LVI

I think I see and hear—but there
Is naught of earth and naught of air
That interests or touches me,
Or moves my sullen apathy,
Save as it proves—a smell, a cry,
A bell—to my sad spirit, seeing,
Sensing—or a mere passerby—
The arabesque that is your being...

LVII

Dans cette infinité, dans cette plénitude
Qui composent le corps courageux et maudit,
Malgré les maux mortels, malgré la servitude,
On sent toujours latent un secret paradis...

LVII

Limitless flesh—courageous, cursed—that fills
This body, servile and yet infinite;
For all its servitude, its mortal ills,
One feels a paradise that lurks in it...

LXVIII

Univers, je t'ai regardé
D'un œil qui loue et qui défie.
J'ai perdu, car tes coups de dés
Ont frappé et vaincu ma vie.
– Mais ce qui fut reste existant:
J'ai fait lutter d'un cœur constant
Ma force avec l'onde et ses voiles,
Mes désirs avec tes printemps,
Et mes yeux avec tes étoiles!

LXVIII

O universe, I looked on you
With praise, and yet distrustfully.
I've lost, for with the dice you threw
You struck my life and bested me.
—But what had been remains, in fact:
I plied my rugged heart, intact
And strong, against seas' wave and sail;
My lust your springtime youth attacked;
My eyes, your stars... And I prevail!

LXIX

Si ta voix m'avait dit: Demeure
Parmi les choses d'ici-bas,
Peut-être ne croirais-je pas
Qu'il faut qu'on meure!

Mais tu t'en fus â pas de loup,
Et muet, sous la morne terre.
Peut-être es-tu, dans ce mystère,
Encor jaloux?

Pourtant, tu désapprends l'envie
Dans le néant sans nul souhait.
Mais ta mort habite ma vie,
Et c'est ma détresse et ma paix
De croire qu'en ton cœur de cire
Tu me désires...

LXIX

Had you but told me, by the by:
Live on among life here below;
Perhaps I'd not believe it so
    That one must die!

But you stole off with wolf-like tread.
Now mute in earth's drear gloom you lie,
Jealous of me, perhaps, that I
    Am not yet dead?

Yet you shun envy's uselessness
In that void where to yearn is vain.
Your death dwells in my life... My pain
Persuades me–in my calm distress–
That you, in your heart's waxen will,
    Desire me still...

LXXI

Je suis où tu es, nulle part.
Ni toi ni moi ne sommes plus!
Je vis vaguement, au hasard,
Sachant que tout est révolu,

Et ce que j'observe et ressens
Ne fait que fixer dans mes yeux
Le livide arrêt de ton sang
Sous l'indifférence des cieux!

LXXI

Nowhere am I, and you as well,
For we exist no more! Life's force
Grows dim... Vague, randomly I dwell
Knowing that all has run its course;

And everything I see and sense
Merely sets clear before my eyes
Your pale blood's quelling turbulence,
Grown still beneath uncaring skies!

LXXX

Jadis je m'aimais,
Tu sais quel orgueil
Parfois animait
Ma voix et mon œil.

– L'esprit sombre et froid,
Je hais moi sans toi.

LXXX

I liked myself back then;
You know how strongly my
Pride would, now and again,
Stir in my voice, my eye.

–Soul dark, cold, "you"–bereft,
I loathe the "me" that's left...

LXXXI

L'homme s'attache à l'espérance
Quand le sort lui fut trop cruel.
Entre les tombes et le ciel
Il fait ondoyer sa souffrance.

– Ô morts, je ne recherche pas
La trace pâle de vos pas;
Je meurs, mais sans vaines tempêtes,
Que d'autres aient de sourds débats
Et lèvent vers les cieux leurs têtes.
Moi, je sais: je vais où vous êtes!

LXXXI

To hopefulness mankind will cling
When fate has dealt a bitter doom.
And, betwixt heaven and the tomb,
He brandishes his suffering.

–O you, departed, I trace not
Your pallid footfalls misbegot;
Calmly I die, untrumpeted.
Let others moan and mourn their lot,
And to the heavens raise sad their head:
Mindful, I join you, my dear dead!

XC

Je n'avais jamais rien à dire
Qu'à toi. Aux autres je parlais
Comme l'on se meut ou respire,
Mais jamais mon cœur ne mêlait
Son trésor à leur existence.
Nous seuls n'avions pas de distance.
Sûrs d'un familier infini,
Nous étions pressés, réunis
Dans l'étroitesse ou dans l'espace.
En toi seul j'étais à ma place.

Que veux-tu que la gloire soit,
Si ce n'est l'image de soi
Dans l'âme que l'on a choisie?
L'offrande de la poésie,
Je la faisais à ton regard.
Ce n'était que dans ta prunelle
Que j'étais juste et naturelle.
Désormais sans vœux, sans égards,
Je suis cette errante hirondelle
Dont on voit sur l'azur hagard
Se déchirer les noirs coups d'ailes...

XC

Never had I a thing to say
To others, only you. And when
I spoke to them now and again
It was just in an offhand way–
Like breathing, walking; but my heart,
Spurning them, held its wealth apart.
We two alone stood each to each,
Infinite our familiar reach,
Pressed close or spreading wide to space.
In you alone I found my place.

But what is glory? What is it
But the self-image we find fit
To live within the soul we love?
I wrote my poetry, whereof
An offering I made, whereby
Your eyes alone saw me withal,
As nature made me, flaws and all.
Desireless now and aimless, I
Am like the swallow, fluttering free,
Whose darkly flapping wings we see
Scraping the ragged azure sky...

CV

J'ai dormi, j'ai pendant quelques instants rejoint
La vide immensité où ne se trouvent point
Ni ton sort, arrêté, ni le mien, continu.
– J'ai reposé sous l'arc interminable et nu
Où tout être s'ignore avant, après la vie.
En quittant ce néant, je porte au cœur l'envie
De retourner sans fin vers ce suave site
Dont j'eus en m'éveillant le contact et le goût.

– Les ténèbres! l'oubli! Plus rien, ni moi, ni vous!
Lieu d'avant la naissance, unique réussite!

CV

I slept, and for a moment joined that vast
Void, where neither my present nor your past
Abide; where every creature that draws breath
Is mystery—before life, after death:
—Beneath its timeless vaulting arch I lay;
My heart yearned, as I quit that void, to stay
Endlessly in its gentle nothingness
That still I savored, sensed, when sleep was done.

—You? Me? No, nothing! Shades! Oblivion!
That space before our birth, life's lone success!

DERNIERS VERS

(1933 [posth.])

MISSION

J'ai reçu dans mes yeux le jeune éclat du jour
En sentant mon plaisir moins sacré que ma tâche;
Repoussant les repos heureux, j'ai, sans relâche,
Exalté l'univers et le perfide amour.

– Et tu m'avais choisie, ô Monde, pour transmettre
À ce vague infini qui semble t'intriguer,
Et que l'homme poursuit par d'innombrables guets,
Le secret éclairci des choses et des êtres.

J'accomplissais la dure et noble mission:
Le rêve, la douleur, l'effort, la passion,
L'horizon coloré, les grâces naturelles
Envahissaient mon âme et se fiaient â elle
Pour que rien ne pérît du véhément trésor...
Je fus l'asile sûr, l'activité du port,
Le lien palpitant de la terre à la nue,
Le négoce divin par qui tout continue!

– Vous que je porte en moi, flamme, azur, océan,
Puisque je vais mourir, que dirai-je au néant?

MISSION

Eyes filled with dawn's bright gleam, I thought more of
My sacred task than pleasure's joys. I spurned
Contentment and repose; incense I burned
Before the universe and faithless love.

–You chose me, World, so that I might transmit
That secret of beings and things–that man
Pursues from port to port as best he can–
Unto the vague, intriguing infinite.

I carried out the arduous, noble mission:
Dream, suffering and pain, passion, ambition,
All Nature's grace, the far horizon's hues
Beset my soul, trusted it, loath to lose
Any part of life's lusty pleasure pure...
I was the teeming port, the refuge sure,
Throbbing link that joined earth to heaven anon,
Commerce divine whereby this life goes on!

–You, of my flesh: flame, ocean, azure sky–
What shall I tell the void now that I die?

REPROCHE

Qu'importe que dans l'ombre existent
Ces beaux astres brillants et tristes
Dont les feux ne connaîtront rien
De leur empire aérien!
Mais que mon regard les assiste,
Que mon rêve, ample et soucieux,
Veuille parer mon corps qui passe
Des vastes bijoux de l'espace;
Que mon œil, habitant des cieux,
Erre sur cette piste immense
Où rien ne cesse, ne commence,
Alors que la chair et l'esprit
Vont par la mort être surpris
Et quitter leur fière démence,
Ô Monde insensible et distrait,
Pour qui rien n'est utile ou vrai,
Dans la nuit respirante et fraîche
Voilà l'injurieuse flèche!

REPROACH

What matters that, gloom-fraught, afar
Shines many a sad and beauteous star,
Whose fires have no idea at all
Of the power wrought by them withal!
How much in need of me they are–
My generous dream, my probing eyes!
Ah! Let my transient body's grace
Sport the lush gems that sprinkle space;
And let my gaze wander the skies
Over broad fields of nothingness–
The endless, the beginingless–
As flesh and spirit, lingering there,
Will be caught dead and unaware,
Proud no more of life's mad *noblesse*...
O World unfeeling, thought-bereft,
For whom no useful truths are left,
In night's cool and refreshing breath,
This, the dart's sting that deals us death.

OBSESSION

L'enclos qui te retient, le tombeau qui t'opprime,
Je les vois en tous lieux.
Je crois que c'est l'azur, les chemins et la cime
Qui recouvrent tes yeux.

Tu dors sous l'univers, le corps détruit, la face
Plongeant dans la torpeur,
Et moi, errante encor, quelque pas que je fasse,
Je marche sur ton cœur!

OBSESSION

Oppressive space, the grave where you lie still:
        I see them everywhere.
Over your eyes I sense the roads, the hill,
        Even the azured air.

You sleep the universe, flesh moldering,
        Stare fixed in torpor, dead...
And I, with every step, still wandering,
        Upon your heart I tread!

RÉSIGNATION

Quand on a tant aimé, tant loué l'univers,
Et que l'immense azur et l'éclatement vert
Viennent rompre avec nous les grandes fiançailles,
On combat, on languit. L'inégale bataille
Irrite en notre esprit l'affront d'avoir vécu.
Puis, lassé de souffrir, épuisé, juste et chaste,
Le cœur conçoit enfin, avec un sens aigu,
L'innocence du sort, favorable ou néfaste,
Et l'esprit, dédaignant ce qui lui semblait dû
Contemple calmement le monde hostile et vaste,
Où l'homme, hôte pensif, n'était pas attendu!

RESIGNATION

When we have wooed the universe and been
Spurned by the blue expanse and bursts of green
That gainsay our betrothal, though the foe
Ply arms unequal, still we face our woe
At having lived, and fight though all is ended.
Our weary heart, paining yet worse and worse–
Just, pure–at last has clearly comprehended
Fate's blameless innocence–a boon? a curse?
Mind scorns its seeming due and, unoffended,
Gazes, calm, at a hostile universe,
Where man, the thoughtful guest, came unintended.

CONTEMPLATION

Je regarde les cieux: un fracas de lumière
Émane du soleil, sa turbulente essence
Dans l'azur infini joyeusement élance
Le séculaire appel et la force première.
Et puis l'ombre survient. La nocturne pâleur
Autant que l'or du jour intrigue le regard;
On voit errer au ciel l'inflexible hasard
Dans la pulsation des étoiles en pleurs.
Nul amour, nul secours, nulle miséricorde
De l'abîme d'en haut sur l'homme ne s'abaisse.
L'effrayant univers l'ignore et le déborde.
Vanité de l'espoir! ô stoïque paresse!
Vous envahissez l'être et vous rendez oisif
L'esprit toujours trahi par l'espace insensé.
– Et c'est l'étonnement d'un front contemplatif
Qu'on puisse écrire encore après avoir pensé!

CONTEMPLATION

I gaze the heavens: light bursts clangorously
Out of the sun; primal force, turbulent,
Calls, joyous, through the azure firmament
Over the course of many a century.
Then the night-pallor settles, shadows rise,
No less than day's bright gold, luring our gaze;
We see unbending fate wander the skies
To the pulse of the weeping stars. We raise
From depth's abysses to the heavens' height
No tender pity, love of humankind;
Nor succor for man's torment can we find.
The frightening universe ignores man, quite,
Trammels him... Hope? Vain! Stoic idleness!
Mind gulled by space forever passionless...
–And, pensive-browed, astonished that one might,
For all one's thought, be able still to write!

"LE SOMMEIL M'ENVAHIT..."

Le sommeil m'envahit, je suis lucide encor.
La torpeur, dans ma main, descend comme une rose.
Je palpe, ainsi qu'un roi qui tient un globe d'or,
Le monde inférieur sur qui je me repose.

Mon esprit soulevé dédaigne ce qui fut.
Nul souvenir du jour, plus de mémoire amère;
Magnanime oiseleur délaissant ses affûts,
Le temps m'accorde un pur mépris de l'éphémère!

Augustes sentiments au rebut: gloire, amour,
Combat de tout instant pour trouver dans les hommes
L'enchantement secret, cet étrange secours
Qui menace, accomplit, détruit ce que nous sommes,

Vous n'êtes plus qu'un fin tourbillon dans mon sang!
L'excès et la langueur guérissent d'être avide.
Le soir qui s'obscurcit n'est soudain qu'un absent.
Et je contemple, avec un œil épris du vide,
Le délicat regard qu'ouvre en la nuit solide
La fêlure aérée et pure du croissant!

“SLEEP RUSHES OVER ME...”

Sleep rushes over me; lucid, I linger
Yet... In my hand falls torpor, gentle rose.
Like the king with a globe of gold, I finger
This lesser world below, where I repose.

My spirit, raised, disdains what was. There is
No memory of the day, no bitterness:
Bird-catcher kind, quitting those lures of his,
Time lets me scorn what little lasts, or less.

Glory, love... August sentiments put by–
Unceasing struggle waged to find in men
That secret charm that works its succor wry,
That threatens, makes us whole, destroys us then–

Now but a whirlwind in my blood are you!
Languor and lust’s excesses, cured at last.
Suddenly evening flits, flees, hides from view.
Charmed by the void, I stare at night–amassed,
Solid–but that the moon’s soft glance, pure-cast
In crescent gaze, splits airily in two!

“LES JOURS ONT FUI...”

Les jours ont fui. Qu’est-ce qui peut changer?
Vos os toujours sont au sol mélangés.
Le temps sur moi, d’un pas régulier,
Meurtrit un cœur à tout mésallié.
Je hais en vous, espace aérien,
L’été si dur à qui n’espère rien!
Partout où l’homme a placé l’infini,
Je n’aperçois que de basses cloisons.
La verte branche où va mûrir le nid
Sera rompue en la froide saison.
Le sort sanglant accable et désunit
Ce que nouaient l’amour et la raison.
– Et sous le ciel où tout est bref et vain,
Je fus cet œil, plein d’un songe divin!

"THE DAYS HAVE FLOWN..."

The days have flown, what can now yet be changed?
Your bones still lie, fusing with earth. On me,
Time, with its trampling pace, treads heavily,
Bruising a heart from everything estranged.
Huge realm of space, I loathe your summer! Dead
At last its hopefulness! For now, wherever
Man once would place his faith in the forever–
The infinite–my eye sees nothing spread
But lowly walls. The green branch where the nest
Would thrive and grow, will–brief, vain as the rest!–
Be broken here below by winter's breath:
Bloody fate sunders to a separate death
Whatever love and reason would combine...
–I was that eye, filled with a dream divine!

ÉGALITÉ

Les lieux qui vous sont bons sont bons aussi pour moi,
Je n'ai jamais aimé que l'abondant partage.
Puisque vos corps éteints sont retranchés des mois,
Je suis absente aussi des séjours et des âges!

Le petit univers qui porte nos fiertés,
Qui tolère un instant nos vœux et nos audaces,
Et nous concède un bref empire dans l'espace,
Aux instants du désir et de la volupté,

Je n'en peux plus aimer le négligent visage!
– Cieux qui m'ont enivrée, étroit monde natal,
À présent que je vois se hâter mon passage,
J'absous le fol destin, inutile et fatal.

– Et de tout ce qui fut mon extase et mon zèle,
Ma force opiniâtre et mon multiple amour,
De tout ce qui faisait que, mince entre mes ailes,
Je frémissais, pensante abeille de velours,

Il ne me reste plus, sauf le bonheur du somme,
Que ces instants légers, sans souhaits, sans espoir,
Où j'aime encor ce front que désiraient les hommes,
Lorsque d'un pas dansant je pénètre un miroir...

EQUALITY

The places you deem good are good for me;
Ever my wish: to share the boon somehow.
But since your bodies quit time's panoply–
Wrenched dead–I too have quit the here-and-now!

The petty universe that bears our pride
Brooks, but an instant, what we dare desire;
Allows us scant dominion–grudging, snide–
Over space, when burns brief our bliss's fire:

No, I can love no more its spurning face!
–O skies that made me drunk, birth-world confining,
Now that I see my steps rush on apace,
I pardon mad fate's futile death, resigning.

And, of all that was once my ecstasy,
My headstrong zeal, love many-faceted–
Of all that made me, like some thinking bee,
Wee, velvet creature, quiver, wings outspread–

Naught have I left but sleep's contentment, where
Instants–my hopes now fled–will, weightless, pass;
Where I love still this brow that men found fair,
As, dreaming, I dance through the looking-glass...

CHLOÉ

Petit poème pour une anthologie.

Chloé, timide enfant, ô vierge chevrière,
Dont le voluptueux et chaste étonnement
Fera rêver sans fin l'audace des amants,
Toi dont le nom retient l'amour et la lumière,

Que devint ton destin quand te fut révélé
L'envahissant plaisir qui suspend ton haleine?
As-tu vécu sans pleurs, ton doux corps emmêlé
Au pâtre qui t'apprit ses jeux dans Mytilène?

N'as-tu jamais connu le désordre et les maux
Du désir, cris d'oiseaux et lancinantes ailes,
Quand le printemps furtif, sur les sombres rameaux,
Fait soudain crépiter ses vertes étincelles?

Dans ton île pierreuse où le cyprès touffu
Semble un mât préparé pour déployer sa voile
Et voguer vers la vaine énigme des étoiles,
As-tu su demeurer la nymphe que tu fus?

Ton agreste bonheur, près des purs asphodèles,
Des troupeaux turbulents et des flots aux beaux plis,
A-t-il pu te garder, Chloé, d'être infidèle,
Et de louer Eros au creux d'un nouveau lit?

Qu'importe! Rien ne peut arrêter ta jeunesse,
Ton regard ingénu que bombe un frais cristal;
Tu reposes, pudique, ô gracile déesse!
Dans le constant azur d'un roman pastoral.

CHLOE

Little poem for an anthology

O Chloe, timid virgin, goat-girl sprite
Whose chaste awe and naïve voluptuousness
Make endless lovers dream of bold excess;
You, whose mere name echoes with love and light...

What was your fate? Did you weep as you yearned
In newfound panting pleasure, ardent-fleshed,
With Mytilene's shepherd-lad enmeshed,
Body to body, as his games you learned?

What? Did you never know lust's chaos, woes,
The cries of birds, the throbbing, pain-wracked wings
When spring, on somber branch, in stealthy pose,
Suddenly sparkles its green sputterings?

On your stone isle, where tufted cypress, thin
And tall–like mast about to spread its sail
And seek the riddling stars, to no avail–
Could you remain the nymph that you had been?

Has rustic joy, Chloe–daffodils pure,
The flocks frolicking free, the billowing waves–
Kept you from being the faithless paramour
In praise of Eros, bedded by new knaves?

No matter! Nothing can cut short your youth
Or dull the crystal that swells, fresh, your glance;
Shyness-graced goddess! Yours, the constant truth
Of pastoral tale's azure-vast expanse.

CHLOE. See note, p. 197.

Line 8: The Greek isle of Mytilène is the setting of Chloé's and Daphnis's pastoral amours. (Trans.)

CHATTE PERSANE

La chambre, où l'été monotone
Confine les ors de sa gloire.
Une brise tiède frissonne
Et creuse d'argentines moires
Sur la chatte aux yeux de démone
Qui, sournoise et longue, vient boire
Dans le vase des anémones...

PERSIAN CAT

Bedchamber... Boring summer's frieze
Of glorious gold... And, by and by,
Quivering warm, a silvered breeze
Shimmers the cat—she of the eye
Demonic!—lithe, who, if you please,
Laps from the long vase—ah, so sly!—
The one filled with anemones...

LES ÎLES BIENHEUREUSES

I

Onde, ciel frais glissant avec de claires ailes
Dans les prés, et portant de chantantes nouvelles,
Sans vous le paysage a ses yeux las et clos!
Les cœurs, comme la soif, ont le désir de l'eau.
Toute chose qui plaît a sa source légère:
Le branchage et les fleurs sont de sucre humectés,
Les fruits laissent filtrer un parfum qui suggère
Le suave torrent dans Ieur chair arrêté.
La ceinture des flots rend les îles divines,
Et, dans la plus obscure et morose cité,
L'esprit est réjoui dès l'instant qu'il devine
Le chant de la fontaine, au jet précipité...

THE HAPPY ISLES

I

Waves, cool sky gliding over fields on wings
Clear and bright, singing news of happenings
Galore. If not for you, the landscape's eyes,
Weary, would be shut tight! The water lies
Eager to slake hearts' thirst, here, there; yearned-for
Water, light birth of fair things everywhere...
Flower and branch lie sugar-moist; what's more,
Fruits' flesh-perfumes go seeping, devil-may-care,
In gentle flood. The water girdles round
The heavenly isles; no quarter drear is there–
Or darkly glum–where joy fails to abound
When waterspout sings out, flailing the air...

II

Île inventée, avec son végétal panache,
Sa moite floraison d'océan qui s'attache
Au sol, et largement l'humecte de bonheur!
Corail sur l'arbrisseau, coquillages en fleur
Qui semblent attentifs, ainsi que la gazelle,
Aux pudiques secrets que se disent entre elles
Les filles du jardin, graves comme des sœurs.
– Nous ne connaîtrons pas la flambante prairie
Où s'écoulent les jours étincelants, égaux.
L'image éveille en nous un nostalgique écho.
– Dans l'arome du vent qui s'élève des flots,
Que n'ai-je pu rêver sous une draperie,
Mollement suspendue aux palmiers indigos!

II

Pleasure-invented, flora-tufted isle,
Whose ocean, flowering a happy smile,
Clings to it, sprinkling its moist happiness!
Coral-clung bushes, shells in bloom, that press
An eager ear, gazelle-like, to the stream
Of secrets that the garden-wenches seem—
Blameless as nuns!—to banter, passionless.
—That flaming strand cannot be ours to know,
Where, sparkling, each the same, days calmly flow...
—Ah! In the waves' aroma, what would I
Not dream, nostalgia-fraught, could I but lie
Gently beneath a sheet, spread by the by,
And swaying in the palm-trees' indigo!

III

Écailleuse rondeur à quoi tout s'évertue:
Le flot, les fleurs, le roc, l'arbre à noix de cocos;
Le petit voilier dur est en dos de tortue,
L'eau se hausse et se traîne en course d'escargots.
– Ah! pouvoir habiter vraiment ce paysage,
Pouvoir, quand tout nous nuit, poser sur le visage
Du nonchalant, maussade et constant univers,
Ce masque somptueux, bleu, violet et vert!

III

Turtle-scale seaside bulge, sole cynosure
Of waves, coconut tree, flowers, craggy cliff,
Tortoise-shell hull of little sailing skiff,
Rising tide's snail-wise pace... Oh, to immure
Ourselves within the beauties of this place
When life mistreats us, and to hide the face
Of dour, uncaring, cosmic go-betweens
With mask of sumptuous violets, blues, and greens!

IV

Dans les joyaux touffus et animés du val,
Où le feuillage autant que le plumage ondule,
Est-ce l'aube intriguée ou le soir estival?
Énigme du matin ou bien du crépuscule?
On goûte le tranquille et sensuel bonheur
Que le silence épand au milieu des couleurs,
Dans l'arome qui sourd des moelleuses capsules.
– Et devant le secret du parfum pictural,
Je me souviens du cri de Gérard de Nerval,
Où l'on ne sait quel feu mystérieux circule:
« Rose au cœur violet, fleur de sainte Gudule! »

IV

There, midst the valley's gems–lush, spirited–
Where swaying greenery and plumage pose,
Is it the dawn, poking her curious head,
Or summer eve? Morning or dusk, in throes
Of an enigma? Sensuous, tranquil taste
Of silent joy, with vibrant colors laced,
Scents seeping blossom-soft... And, as it grows
More dense in pictured fragrance subtly spread,
Gérard de Nerval's cry rings in my head,
Fired with mysterious meaning no one knows:
"Violet-hearted, Saint Gudula's rose!"

Line 11: The enigmatic line quoted is from "Artémis," one of the sonnets of Nerval's "Les Chimères." Gudula, a seventh-century saint, is venerated in the Lowlands, and particularly as the patroness of Brussels. The "rose" referred to may possibly be an allusion to a flower, the *tremella deliquescens,* known as "Saint Gudula's lantern" (for reasons that stem from an episode in her iconography), though, like the *rose trémière* (hollyhock), also mentioned in "Artémis," it is not a rose at all. Nerval scholars, literati, and religious commentators have attempted a variety of explanations. (Trans.)

MIRAGE DE NOËL

Plus que l'été d'azur et d'ambre,
J'ai, dans l'enfance, aimé le gel
Du soir ténébreux de Noël
Et le vert sapin dans la chambre.

J'imaginais l'âne et le bœuf
Attiédissant l'ombre glacée,
Les mages, l'étoile empressée,
L'enfant, arrondi comme l'œuf

Du Saint-Esprit, ramier céleste,
Et dont le mystique baiser
S'était divinement posé
Sur la Vierge sainte et modeste.

Que de froidure! que de vent!
Et le tremblement de la porte!...
Puis, soudain, un roi blanc apporte
Son cadeau d'or. Le roi suivant

Est blanc encore,–mais le troisième
Est un roi noir. J'avais si peur
Qu'il eût honte de sa couleur!
Mais je voyais l'enfant suprême

Accueillir le bon nègre aussi
De son sourire qui protège!
– À présent, je songe au souci
Que m'eût causé, parmi la neige

Qui brillait en mon cœur, le net
Azur baignant les molles palmes,
(Et nul sapin!) pendant le calme
Et chaud Noël de Nazareth!

CHRISTMAS VISION

More than the summer's azure-gold
I loved the frost, all shadow-spread
In childhood Christmases of old,
And the green fir tree by the bed.

I mused on ox, ass, warming mild
The ice-chilled shade; the star on high
Coursing its path through evening sky,
Guiding the Magi; and the child,

Plump as a dove's egg, Spirit-blessed—
Celestial dove, heavenly graced—
Whose kiss divine was gently placed
On modest Virgin's holy breast.

How cold it is! The wind bursts through,
Rattles the door!... Then, suddenly,
A white king makes his way, and he
Brings gift of gold... The next, white too...

At length, the third king in my dream
Is black, and I am quite afraid
Lest he, alas, might rue the shade
His skin is in! But the supreme

Babe-god welcomed this black no less
With his sweet, all-protecting smile!
—And I dream of the snows the while,
And of the wintertime duress

Shining bright in my heart: the breath
Of deep blue swathing leaves of palm—
No fir tree here!—during the calm,
Warm Christmastide of Nazareth!

SAGESSE

Vis sans peur, sans remords et sans contrainte. Crains
De dépasser les jours consacrés aux caresses,
Puisque tout n'aboutit qu'au lit où l'on étreint,
Qu'à la tombe où l'on cesse!

WISDOM

Live fearless, guiltless, free. Fear only lest
You spend more days embracing than one ought:
All ends in bed–caressing and caressed–
    And in the grave, where all is naught!

L'ANCÊTRE

à M. Jean Rostand.

D'où sommes-nous venus, quel est l'ancêtre étrange,
L'agreste, inconscient et lascif animal,
Qui, séparant un jour le bien d'avec le mal,
Fit naître en nous l'angoisse et la pudeur de l'ange?

À quel moment du temps, comme en quelle saison,
Le désir, qui guidait ses gambades heureuses,
Fit-il place à l'ardeur pensive et langoureuse
Et fixa-t-il en nous la solide raison?

Habitant des forêts ou bien des mers fécondes,
Sombre aïeul séculaire, endormi sans remords,
Par qui nous connaissons le plaisir et la mort,
À travers la douleur infuse dans le monde,

Je songe à tes yeux prompts, à tes gais appétits,
À tes crimes prudents, peureux et nécessaires,
Et je lève mon front, hanté de paradis,
Vers la nue où jamais tes vœux ne se posèrent.

THE ANCESTOR

For M. Jean Rostand

Where do we come from? Who, that strange, debased
Ancestor, mindless beast roaming the wood,
Who, one day, learned to tell evil from good,
Bred anguish and angelic honor chaste?

In what moment of time, what season, was
That lust that spawned his wanton revelry
Replaced by pensive longing? When did he
Fix on our languorous soul staunch reason's laws?

Denizen of the forests or lush seas,
You taught us death and pleasure; now you sleep
Without remorse, you who the wide world steep
In woe, dark forebear of the centuries.

I dream your sharp look, giddy appetites—
Misdeeds essential, fear-wrought, worldly-wise;
Paradise-plagued, I raise my brow toward heights
Unyearned-for, where you never turned your eyes.

Dedication: Noted biologist, scientific popularizer, and member of the Académie Française, Jean Rostand (1894–1977) was the son of famous playwright Edmond Rostand and poet Rosemonde Gérard. Though an outspoken freethinker and pro-evolutionist, as implied in Noailles' dedication, he hardly deserves her gentle suggestion that he sacrificed moral scruple to science. On the contrary, he was active in many ethical causes, among them the campaigns against nuclear armament and capital punishment. (Trans.)

TÉNACITÉ

Le jour morne est d'un jour morne encore suivi.
Brave et tenace au cours du chemin monotone,
Le corps rêveur escompte un bonheur qui l'étonne:
Pour ce peu de bonheur que l'on espère, on vit!

On vit pour cet instant sans bord, mais éphémère:
Ambition, triomphe, amour, insanité!
Pour ce trop fort plaisir, ce peu de volupté,
Nulle obstination ne semble trop amère.

Pourtant, tout redescend vers l'angoisse ou l'oubli.
L'homme ne garde pas ses superbes conquêtes,
Il n'est pas de lueur que le destin n'arrête.
– Amants, qui triomphez dans l'ouragan des lits,

Et déchiffrez soudain par l'ivresse secrète
Qui livre l'infini à vos tendres délits,
Les plans universels par quoi le monde existe,
Que j'aime votre extase, ample, savante et triste!

TENACITY

Sullen day follows day, sullen no less.
Stubborn, along our route of dull ennui,
We dream of sudden pleasure, eagerly,
And live for that brief, hoped-for happiness!

We live for that one instant's termless love,
Ambition, triumph, madness... Endless, but
Only a trice; and, obstinate, we glut
On the utter and bitter bliss thereof!

But all will be forgot, or fall to dust
Or pain; man cannot long retain his grand
Triumphs: no glimmer spared by fate's fell hand!
—Lovers, who best beds' hurricanes, you must

Discover, by what drunken secret—planned
To render infinite your tender lust
And spawn the world's boundless complexity—
How I love your vast, shrewd, sad ecstasy!

EXIGENCE

L'être recherche le plaisir,
Toute sa force le réclame,
Nous conférons le beau nom d'âme
À la puissance du désir.

Il faudrait que toujours nous tente
Quelque appel ou bien quelque attente,
Et, repoussant le morne effort
Qu'exige la vie humble et creuse,
L'homme se ruerait vers la mort,
S'il la savait voluptueuse.

DEMANDS

The human creature has one goal,
Pleasure: he yearns for it, unending;
Beautiful is that name, "the soul",
We give to our desires unbending.

Something must always be, that should
Call to us, tempt us; and man would
Reject the effort, still the breath
Of this drear, hollow life of his,
And would go chasing even death
If he were sure what bliss it is.

CONSCIENCE

Quand le sort semble pur et franc
Et que la jeunesse s'efforce,
Comme la sève sous l'écorce,
À dominer le corps souffrant,
Périr paraît inique et lâche;
On s'acharne à la dure tâche,
Comme un travailleur dans le rang.

J'ai craint d'avoir tort en mourant.

CONSCIENCE

When life is pure and hope is high,
And youth strives hard, like sap within
The bark, to conquer pain's chagrin,
Subdue the body, then, to lie
Undone and dead seems a disgrace;
Workman-like, one assumes one's place,
Attacks the task, and asks not why.

I feared that I was wrong to die.

CONCLUSION

Calme désertion, dénouement faible et tendre;
Pour tout ce qu'on briguait, indolence et mépris;
Corps inerte, apaisé, où l'on sent se détendre
Tout ce qu'offrait la vie et qui faisait son prix.

Laissez-moi m'endormir, sommeiller c'est connaître,
C'est être nettement et justement savant.
La mort, par son opaque et mystique fenêtre,
Ne laisse plus passer rien qui soit décevant.

L'immense vanité qui comblait nos journées,
Les risibles combats pour devancer autrui,
Les souffrances du corps laissant l'âme étonnée,
La foule des regrets vont finir aujourd'hui!

La terre sans pitié que seul rend excusable
Le frémissant désir de se perpétuer,
Étroitement prendra dans le froid de son sable
L'un de ceux qui naquit afin d'être tué.

CONCLUSION

Weak, gentle denouement... Abandonment
Of all we plotted, all our indolence,
Our scorn; body inert, at peace; now spent,
All that gave life its value and its sense.

Let me sleep, for in sleep alone we take
Knowledge's fitting measure, generous.
Death, through its window, mystic and opaque,
Lets nothing pass that might ill-temper us.

The vanity immense that filled our days,
Laughable combats to gain victories,
Pain of the flesh that would the soul amaze,
The welter of regrets... Gone now all these!

Cruel earth, absolved by feverish desire
To live anon... In the tight clasp, death-chilled,
Of its cold sand, it will embrace entire
A creature who was born but to be killed.

INDIGENCE

On aime tristement; même à travers la joie,
Un invisible obstacle aisément se déploie
Et disjoint les esprits qui se veulent mêler.
Hélas! tout être est seul sous le ciel étoilé!
L'orgueil a son désert ainsi que sa tendresse.
Douleur du noble amour ou de l'ambition,
Vous voyez fuir l'espoir et languir l'allégresse!
– Pourquoi faut-il que l'âpre et brève passion
Où l'homme s'assouvit, se limite et s'abaisse,
De tous les sentiments soit le seul sans tristesse?

INDIGENCE

Sadly we love; even in joy there lurks
An obstacle unseen, whose evil works
To sunder those spirits on union bent.
Alas! Beneath the star-clad firmament
Each of us stands alone! Pride is no less
A desert than a wealth of tenderness.
O pain of noble love, O strong desire,
Fleeting is hope, happiness all too brief.
—Why not? Why ought the passing passion-fire
That humbles man, and where he finds relief,
Be the one sentiment that knows no grief?

IRRUPTION

Le malheur entre dans la chambre.
Depuis des siècles, il accourt,
Il brise le cœur et les membres;
L'être stoïque est sans recours
Contre cet hôte turbulent,
Qui, tantôt hâtif, tantôt lent,
Nous guide vers la tombe étrange
Où la vie, avec son cœur d'ange,
Ne trouve plus aucun amour.
– Ô mort preste, élan sans échange,
Cassure abrupte dans le jour!

IRRUPTION

For centuries death roams. See him
Come running through the chamber door!
Now sore of heart, broken of limb,
Stoic, we let the conqueror
Against whom there is no defense
Lead us on, through his turbulence,
To the strange tomb—now fast, now slow—
Where life, once angel-hearted, lo!
Finds no more love to hunger for.
—Death, spry, quick, with no quid pro quo:
Mere interruption, nothing more!

CONFRONTATION

À l'horizon pâli du matin automnal,
Je regarde à travers le fin rideau d'un saule,
Le coteau délicat comme une mince épaule,
Qu'un oiseau frôle avec son doux ventre animal.

La nature se meurt. Sa grâce reposée,
Où rêvent dignement des larmes en suspens,
Ne semble pas tourner vers le flambant dieu Pan
Ses yeux qu'éblouissaient les caresses osées.

Ce qui fléchit en elle expire mollement.
Même quand le verger et la vigne rougeoient,
Elle ne s'unit plus à cette pourpre joie
Qui mêlait en été la bacchante et l'amant.

Sa sereine faiblesse a bien la connaissance
D'un sommeil où le germe, insidieusement,
Conservant sa vigueur, sa grâce et son essence,
Renaîtra, frais et pur, palpitant diamant.

– Qu'êtes-vous, race humaine, auprès de tant de force!
Parasites rêveurs que grandissait l'esprit,
Vos labeurs, vos espoirs et la stoïque écorce
Dont tout être se vêt, n'empêchent le mépris
D'un monde sans pensers où vos pleurs et vos gestes
Se perdent dans l'espace et les tombes agrestes!

CONFRONTATION

On autumn's dim morning-horizon, gazing
Through a sparse willow-curtain, I see there
The tender slope, like a slim shoulder, where
Flits a soft-bellied bird, flesh gently grazing...

Nature is dying. Stilled, her gracefulness's
Tears are held back: she dreams in dignity,
Seems to ignore Pan's godly flames, as he
Would dazzle her with his daring caresses.

Slowly, softly, her waning will expires.
Even as vine and orchard glow, ignited,
She spurns the crimson joys that had united
Maenad and lover in the summer fires.

Weakly serene, she knows that sleep, for sure,
Will guard intact and surreptitiously
Her essence, vigor, grace; that she will be
Reborn afresh, a diamond, quivering, pure.

–What are you, human race, faced with such force!
Parasite dreamers, aggrandized by mind,
Hopes, labors, and that stoic shell, resource
Of futile use, yet worn by all your kind
Against things' soulless scorn: the tears you weep
Lie lost in space and Nature's graveyard sleep!

Lines 13-16: I've seen no particular reason to follow the poet in her deviation from her established rhyme scheme, a practice not infrequent in her work. (Trans.)

ESPACE

Lorsque le soir est beau, quand sa mince apparence,
Son néant constellé intrigue un cœur savant,
Et quand le monde vert des feuillages balance
Cette odeur de fraîcheur qui compose le vent,

J'absorbe, ayant tout bu dans de divers calices,
La liqueur du triomphe et le venin du fiel,
Ce tout premier bonheur candide et sensuel
De respirer l'éther agile, espiègle et lisse,

Ce tout premier plaisir, celui par qui l'on vit,
Celui par qui l'on songe et pressent l'aventure,
Dont l'allègre vigueur, sitôt qu'on la ravit,
Abandonne à la mort la fière créature.

Beauté de l'air, c'est vous qui fîtes mes pensers.
Vous m'apportiez le monde, ô caresseur des astres!
Votre céleste souffle en tous lieux dépensé,
Amplifiait la joie et calmait les désastres.

Preste organisateur de toutes les saisons,
Ce que vous dédaignez se flétrit et s'efface,
Et je songe à ce jour, calme, dans ma maison,
Où ne recevant plus vos faveurs de l'espace,
J'aurai fermé mon corps, las des cieux et des sons,
Aux douleurs de l'effort comme de la raison.

SPACE

When evening, in its slim design, looms fair,
Its star-swept void thrills the wise heart with wonder;
And, when green leaf and branch spread cool the air
Fresh-scented, everywhere–round, over, under–

I sip–who quaffed from many a chalice, I
Who drank the draught of triumph and life's gall;
That primal, sensuous joy, simplest of all,
Of breathing deep the ether, lithe and sly;

That primal pleasure, life's defining breath
That lets us dream, foretell adventure, whose
Vigor and sprightliness one day we lose,
And that consigns pride's creature to his death.

O star-caresser! Beauteous air unfurled,
You it was, space, who plied my every thought.
Your heavenly breath, blown wide, brought me the world,
Heightened my joys, quelled woes disaster-wrought.

Skilled planner of year's rounds, what you disdain
Ever must wither, fade, and leave no trace;
And I muse on that day when calm will reign,
When I receive no more your favor's grace,
Weary of sky, space, sound, and leave no place
For flesh's strivings and for reason's pain.

DÉPART

J'ai trop lutté, je me résigne.
Quelle circonstance était digne
De tant de souffrances insignes?
Certes les malheurs éclatants
Du corps, de l'âme, sont autant
De témoignages et de signes
Qui parent l'être courageux.

Sache élever au-dessus d'eux
La noblesse d'un col de cygne.

LEAVING

Too much I struggled; now, abject,
Resigned, I yield. Who could expect
Such suffering, unearned, unchecked?
Yes, true it is, the flashing woes
Of flesh and soul are merely those
Proofs that the brave may live bedecked
With emblems of their bravery.

Learn how, in your nobility,
To raise a swan's neck, proud, erect.

“NOUS NE SOMMES JAMAIS TOUT ÉLOIGNÉS…”

Nous ne sommes jamais tout éloignés: la ville,
Où se meut le souci auprès des vanités,
Aborde et se défait près du terrain tranquille
Où tu dors englouti dans la basse cité.

Je ne vais pas te voir, ma douleur souveraine
Ne saurait t'aborder sans partager ton toit.
Ton logis est glacé, ta rue est souterraine,
Le néant que j'anime est étendu sur toi.

J'ai dit que je t'aimais, gaîment, chaque journée,
J'ai vanté cet accord.
Ô Mort tout exultant, qu'a fait la destinée
Des rêves de ton corps?

"NEVER ARE WE APART..."

Never are we apart; the city where
Outskirts furl and unravel in their quest
For vanities chaotic... It is there
That in the peaceful earth you take your rest.

To see you, my majestic anguish must,
Perforce, share your dark roof with you. For, in
A dwelling chill you lie, deep your street's dust,
Beneath the nothingness I live within.

I said I loved you, every day it seems,
          And cheered the ties that bound us.
Exultant Death! Are stilled your flesh's dreams
          By fate hovering round us?

"QUE CRAINS-TU DE QUITTER..."

Que crains-tu de quitter, moribonde enfantine?
Le temps n'aurait pas su changer ton pas dansant,
Et l'étrange vigueur incluse dans ton sang
Eût fait sonner en toi d'éternelles matines.

Se peut-il que tu sois fidèle à l'univers?
D'où te viendrait cette humble et coupable constance?
Ton souffle est emmêlé aux fastes bleus et verts
D'un monde qu'étonnait ta sage turbulence.

Ferme tes larges yeux naïfs et renseignés;
Sois solitaire enfin comme les nobles îles,
Étends paisiblement tes mains d'aspect fragile,
Mais par qui le destin se sentait empoigné
Et renversait vers toi son front aux fortes franges;
Et laisse à ce dur sol où souffrent quelques anges,
Qui maintiendront le feu dont s'embrasait ton cœur,
Son trop peu de désir et son trop peu d'honneur!

“CHILDISH AND DYING...”

Childish and dying, what are you, pray tell,
So loath to leave? Time left your dancing feet
Intact, and your blood’s strangely throbbing heat
Might have rung you a timeless matins-bell.

Is it the universe you’re faithful to?
Whence that guilty and humble constancy?
Your breath is furled in blue-green revelry
Of world awed by the staid, brash likes of you.

Close your wide eyes, naïve, intelligent;
Like the isles, stand alone in noble calm,
Fragile of hand, it seems, but in whose palm
Lay fate, her forehead laced with bangs, head bent;
And leave to earth–where a few angels dwell
In pain, yet who will guard your heart-fires well–
Earth, in its harsh and hard unfeelingness,
Its dearth of love, and honor even less!

"QUAND J'ÉTAIS UNE ENFANT..."

Quand j'étais une enfant, j'aimais sur la colline
M'asseoir dans la chaleur légère des épis
Et voir se bousculer les épaisses brebis
Vers la racine torve et les claires épines.

Mon puéril esprit, qui parcourait le temps,
Me situait parmi les herbes de Sicile,
Et, calme, j'amassais le frais lointain des îles
Où comme moi rêvaient les filles au printemps...

Je me croyais l'enfant que le destin désigne
Pour surveiller le monde et chercher ses secrets,
Et j'ai loyalement, des astres aux forêts,
Observé l'apparence et déchiffré les signes.

Suaves coloris dont l'esprit se repaît!
Plus tard, quand les désirs brisent tout équilibre,
J'ai souvent souhaité retrouver cette paix
De l'enfant méditant près du troupeau qui paît
Et dont l'empressement astucieux et libre
Imprimait au sol vert, par leurs fronts abaissés,
La forme de l'étreinte et celle du baiser.

"WHEN A CHILD..."

When a child, I would take my hillside seat,
And loved to watch the thick-wooled sheep unshorn
Jostle among gnarled root and gleaming thorn
As I sat in the grain-stalks' air-light heat.

My childhood spirit, spanning time a-wing,
Placed me among the grass of Sicily's
Far isle, and I would glean the distant breeze,
Dreaming, with many a lass, of quickening spring...

I thought I was the child that destiny
Handpicked to seek out living's secret sense,
And faithfully plumbed stars and forests, whence
The signs, revealed, would bare themselves to me.

What lissome colors feed the hungering mind!
When, later, lust sundered life's balance, oh!
How I would wish once more that peace to find,
That I, before the grazing sheep, divined,
Gazing upon their freedom, heads bowed low,
Brows in sly homage to the green earth pressed–
Leaving their eager mark–kissed and caressed...

"CELUI QUI MEURT PEUT TOUT..."

Celui qui meurt peut tout enseigner aux vivants.
Immobile, jamais remué par le vent,
Installé dans sa case, accoté à son plâtre,
Il ne voit plus passer ses amis idolâtres,
Et, le regard perdu sous un rêve couvert,
Il contemple le mal rongeant son univers.

Il avait tout prévu dans sa raison agile;
Il savait que le sort n'accorde aucun égard
À l'homme, tout paré de noblesses fragiles,
Dont il blesse le cœur ou l'émail du regard.

Comparant l'étroitesse aux choses infinies,
Il songe à sa naissance où commençaient ses maux
Et déguste l'horreur des longues agonies
En tenant d'un doigt sûr l'effrayant chalumeau.

Il ne dit plus jamais la vérité sonore,
Son ténébreux séjour n'a point d'autre habitant;
Ses solides instincts lentement s'évaporent
Sous l'incertain décret de son geolier, le Temps.

Il avait dépensé la vigueur animale
Et les nobles soucis aux astres accordés,
Sans jamais bien savoir que les heures fatales
Lui destinaient l'étrange et hideux coup de dés.

Le courage est facile aux vivants pleins de rêves;
Un irritable honneur se mêlant à l'amour
Leur apporte un habile et frémissant secours
Qui, lorsqu'ils vont sombrer, les porte et les soulève.

"EVERYTHING LEARN THE LIVING..."

Everything learn the living from one dying.
Never wind-buffeted, in his hut lying
There, by the plaster wall, he scarcely stirs,
Blind to his friends who pass–idolaters
All; and muddling a dream about him furled,
He contemplates the pain that gnaws his world.

He had foreseen it once, in clearer season.
Agile of mind, he knew fate looked askance
At man's noble fragilities–flesh, reason–
Wounding his heart, dulling his polished glance.

Weighing stark life against infinity,
Musing on birth, source of his every woe,
He sips the horror of long agony,
Droned, fingers pressed on sour-toned chalumeau.

Nevermore will he boom the truth; today
His shadow-realm plays host to none but him.
Slowly his solid instincts melt away
Before his jailer Time's commandments dim.

He had spent all his force of living soul,
His nobly caring, boon-bestowed stars' powers,
With no thought that, soon, fate's death-dealing hours
Held for him these strange dice's hideous roll.

Courage daunts not those living, dreamlife-rich;
Honor provoked, but not unmixed with love,
Holds out a hand–clever, though trembling–which,
When they sink low, will lift them high above...

Mais celui dont l'esprit a.trop longtemps lutté,
Oubliant les couleurs des saintes voluptés
Qui furent sa douceur, sa bonté, ses colères,
Fuyant le désarroi de n'aimer plus à plaire,
Tant la douleur du corps a de puissants bourreaux,
Rejoint la mâle paix muette des héros.

But he whose will too long has suffered, whose
Mind forgets those voluptuous, saintly hues
That were sweet, kind, angry at times; who flees
The chaos of no more yearning to please–
So sharp the pains that flesh's hangmen wreak–
Joins heroes' manly calm, and deigns not speak...

Norman R. Shapiro, honored as one of the leading contemporary translators of French, holds the B.A., M.A., and Ph.D. from Harvard University and, as Fulbright scholar, the *Diplôme de Langue et Lettres Françaises* from the Université d'Aix-Marseille. He is Professor of Romance Languages and Literatures at Wesleyan University and is currently Writing and Theater Adviser at Adams House, Harvard University. His many published volumes span the centuries, medieval to modern, and the genres: poetry, novel, and theater. Among them are *Four Farces by Georges Feydeau; The Comedy of Eros: Medieval French Guides to the Art of Love; Selected Poems from Baudelaire's 'Les Fleurs du Mal'; One Hundred and One Poems of Paul Verlaine* (recipient of the Modern Language Association's Scaglione Award); *Negritude: Black Poetry from Africa and the Caribbean;* and *Creole Echoes: The Francophone Poetry of Nineteenth-Century Louisiana.*

A specialist in French fable literature, Shapiro has also published *Fables from Old French: Aesop's Beasts and Bumpkins* and *The Fabulists French: Verse Fables of Nine Centuries.* His translations of La Fontaine are considered by many to be the definitive voicing into English of this famed French poet. His critically acclaimed volumes include *Fifty Fables of La Fontaine; Fifty More Fables of La Fontaine; Once Again, La Fontaine;* and his recent *The Complete Fables of Jean de La Fontaine* for which he was awarded the MLA's prestigious Lewis Galantiere Prize.

His monumental collection *French Women Poets of Nine Centuries: The Distaff and the Pen* won the 2009 National Translation Award from the American Literary Translators Association, as well as two 2008 PROSE Awards from the Association of American Publishers for the Best Single-Volume Reference in the Humanities and Social Sciences and for Excellence in Reference Works.

Other new titles include a completely reset and reillustrated version of *La Fontaine's Bawdy: Of Libertines, Louts, and Lechers; To Speak, to Tell You? Poems by Sabine Sicaud;* and *Préversities: A Jacques Prévert Sampler.* Shapiro is a member of the Academy of American Poets. He was recently named Officier de l'Ordre des Arts et des Lettres de la République Française.

Associate Professor of French and Francophone Studies at the University of Notre Dame, with a Ph.D. from Princeton University, Catherine Perry is also Chevalier in the French national order, "Ordre des palmes académiques," and former Editor-in-Chief of the scholarly journal, *Nouvelles Études Francophones.* Her interests include European intellectual history, gender studies, representations of North Africa in European literature and painting, and Francophone literatures from the Maghreb. Her book, *Persephone Unbound: Dionysian Aesthetics in the Works of Anna de Noailles* (Bucknell UP, 2003), studies Noailles' poetry and prose in relation to philosophical and aesthetic currents in early twentieth-century Europe. She has also published on writers as diverse as Ronsard, Balzac, Stendhal, Proust, Rilke, Valéry, Barrès, Gérard d'Houville, Nicole Brossard, and Malika Oufkir, and she has written an Introduction to *French Women Poets of Nine Centuries: The Distaff and the Pen,* a bilingual anthology of women's poetry in French from the Middle Ages to the present, translated by Norman Shapiro (Baltimore UP, 2008). A resident of Morocco for over ten years, Catherine Perry is interested in Moroccan witness literature, and she is presently studying representations of Islam in contemporary Francophone literature by writers of Muslim origins.

TITLES FROM BLACK WIDOW PRESS

TRANSLATION SERIES

A Life of Poems, Poems of a Life
by Anna de Noailles. Translated by Norman R. Shapiro. Introduction by Catherine Perry.

Approximate Man and Other Writings
by Tristan Tzara. Translated and edited by Mary Ann Caws.

Art Poétique by Guillevic.
Translated by Maureen Smith.

The Big Game by Benjamin Péret.
Translated with an introduction by Marilyn Kallet.

Capital of Pain by Paul Eluard.
Translated by Mary Ann Caws, Patricia Terry, and Nancy Kline.

Chanson Dada: Selected Poems
by Tristan Tzara. Translated with an introduction and essay by Lee Harwood.

Essential Poems and Writings of Joyce Mansour: A Bilingual Anthology
Translated with an introduction by Serge Gavronsky.

Essential Poems and Prose of Jules Laforgue
Translated and edited by Patricia Terry.

Essential Poems and Writings of Robert Desnos: A Bilingual Anthology
Edited with an introduction and essay by Mary Ann Caws.

EyeSeas (Les Ziaux) by Raymond Queneau.
Translated with an introduction by Daniela Hurezanu and Stephen Kessler.

Furor and Mystery & Other Writings
by René Char. Edited and translated by Mary Ann Caws and Nancy Kline.

The Inventor of Love & Other Writings
by Gherasim Luca. Translated by Julian and Laura Semilian. Introduction by Andrei Codrescu. Essay by Petre Răileanu.

La Fontaine's Bawdy
by Jean de La Fontaine. Translated with an introduction by Norman R. Shapiro.

Last Love Poems of Paul Eluard
Translated with an introduction by Marilyn Kallet.

Love, Poetry (L'amour la poésie)
by Paul Eluard. Translated with an essay by Stuart Kendall.

Poems of André Breton: A Bilingual Anthology
Translated with essays by Jean-Pierre Cauvin and Mary Ann Caws.

Poems of A.O. Barnabooth
by Valéry Larbaud. Translated by Ron Padgett and Bill Zavatsky.

Préversities: A Jacques Prévert Sampler
Translated and edited by Norman R. Shapiro.

The Sea and Other Poems by Guillevic.
Translated by Patricia Terry. Introduction by Monique Chefdor.

To Speak, to Tell You?
Poems by Sabine Sicaud. Translated by Norman R. Shapiro. Introduction and notes by Odile Ayral-Clause.

forthcoming translations

Jules Choppin (1830–1914)
New Orleans Poems in Creole and French.
Translated by Norman R. Shapiro.

Poems of Consummation
by Vicente Aleixandre. Translated by Stephen Kessler

MODERN POETRY SERIES

An Alchemist with One Eye on Fire
by Clayton Eshleman

Anticline by Clayton Eshleman

Archaic Design by Clayton Eshleman

Backscatter: New and Selected Poems
by John Olson

The Caveat Onus by Dave Brinks
The complete cycle, four volumes in one.

City Without People: The Katrina Poems
by Niyi Osundare

Concealments and Caprichos
by Jerome Rothenberg

Crusader-Woman by Ruxandra Cesereanu. Translated by Adam J. Sorkin. Introduction by Andrei Codrescu.

Curdled Skulls: Poems of Bernard Bador
Translated by the author with Clayton Eshleman.

Endure: Poems by Bei Dao
Translated by Clayton Eshleman and Lucas Klein.

Exile is My Trade: A Habib Tengour Reader
Translated by Pierre Joris.

Fire Exit by Robert Kelly

Forgiven Submarine
by Ruxandra Cesereanu and Andrei Codrescu

from stone this running by Heller Levinson

The Grindstone of Rapport: A Clayton Eshleman Reader
Forty years of poetry, prose, and translations.

Larynx Galaxy by John Olson

Memory Wing by Bill Lavender

Packing Light: New and Selected Poems
by Marilyn Kallet

The Present Tense of the World: Poems 2000-2009 by Amina Saïd. Translated with an introduction by Marilyn Hacker.

Signal from Draco: New and Selected Poems
by Mebane Robertson

forthcoming modern poetry titles

ABC of Translation by Willis Barnstone

An American Unconscious
by Mebane Robertson

Eye of Witness: A Jerome Rothenberg Reader
Edited with commentaries by Heriberto Yepez & Jerome Rothenberg

Memory by Bernadette Mayer

My Secret Brain: Selected Poems
by Dave Brinks

The Price of Experience
by Clayton Eshleman

LITERARY THEORY / BIOGRAPHY SERIES

Revolution of the Mind: The Life of André Breton by Mark Polizzotti. Revised and augmented edition.